Discovering Piaget
A Guide for Teachers

Richard M. Gorman

CHARLES E. MERRILL PUBLISHING COMPANY
A Bell and Howell Company
Columbus, Ohio

Published by
Charles E. Merrill Publishing Co.
A Bell & Howell Company
Columbus, Ohio 43216

International Standard Book Number: 0-675-09110-1

Library of Congress Catalog Card Number: 77-187715

2 3 4 5 6 7 8 9 10—76 75 74 73 72

Printed in the United States of America

Preface

This introduction to Piaget's thought is designed for use in an education or psychology course. The book can also be read on its own, for it is self-instructional.

Although there are many fine introductions to Piaget available, I have judged that he is worthy of at least one more, particularly one that stresses the school years and applications to education—since his theory has so much to offer for teachers.

If you profit from it, you have many to thank: yourself for becoming involved; Jean Piaget and Bärbel Inhelder for supplying the ideas; my children and others who have served as "subjects"; my colleague Sam Roll for his many penetrating suggestions; many of my students at the University of New Mexico who were part of the revision process; my wife Betty, a colleague in the raising of five children, for supplying the inspiration for the book.

For myself, I am convinced that "to teach is to guide" and with Piaget that "we need students who are active, who learn early to find out by themselves, partly by their own spontaneous activity and partly through material we set up for them." (Piaget, 1964, p. 5) Hopefully, this guided discovery approach to the work of Piaget will help you gain an understanding of his theory as well as some idea of how it might be applied in your teaching.

A
Note
To
The
Reader

A word or two on the format of this book may be in order.

Each chapter is composed of many units or subsections, each set off by a heavy line. Each unit is composed of 1) some expository text or a problem plus sample transcripts, 2) a question, 3) two or three possible answers, and 4) an explanation for each answer.

When you have chosen an answer, simply read the explanation below for that option. If you chose the correct answer, go right on to the next unit; the other explanations are aimed at those who might not have grasped the idea right away.

At the end of each chapter is a review which summarizes the main ideas contained in that chapter. Finally, if at any time throughout the book you are not sure of a term, you will find its definition in the Glossary—Index in the back.

Contents

Chapter 1

Introduction

When is a child intellectually ready to study arithmetic or grammar?

What topics in math and science should be taught at various levels?

On the basis of students' intellectual development, when is it possible to introduce experimental science or foreign language into the curriculum?

What is the best approach or strategy in the teaching of science or social studies on various grade levels?

When is it possible to begin character analysis and the examination of symbolic meaning in the study of literature?

These are some of the questions that developmental psychologists should be able to help teachers and curriculum designers answer. But for years in the United States, psychologists provided very little significant data that could help teachers answer these important questions. Why? Examine the results of a typical study and see if you can discern why.

1

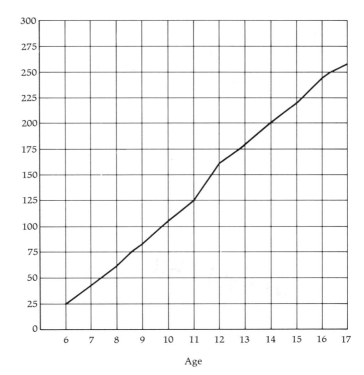

Average Rate of Mental Growth

What can you gain from the above data?

A. Young people get smarter as they grow older.

B. Children are not capable of abstract thinking whereas adolescents
   are.

....

A. Agreed. It's a rather bald way of saying it, but this is what it comes
   down to. For years the main contribution to the educator made by
   psychologists concerned with mental development was that students
   proceed at a rather regular rate of growth—except for a spurt at
   preadolescence; more basically, students are able to answer more
   questions on an intelligence test as they advance in age, with the
   increase found to be relatively steady through the school years.
   Actually, psychologists did derive separate growth curves for such
   varying abilities as memory, spatial relations, word fluency, etc., but
   they were still just growth curves, and they all showed a more or
   less regular pattern of development.

B. There's nothing from the graph that can tell you this. What you would have to do to try to establish that children are not capable of abstract thinking as are adolescents would be to examine the specific test given and see whether the possibility bore out. First of all, it probably wouldn't, and secondly, very few if any teachers actually would go to this trouble. The data only reveals A.

Consider another approach to the study of cognitive development.

The question is asked: "What makes the clouds move?" The children's answers are recorded and then analyzed, and some common characteristics are identified for certain age levels *(on the average)*. The following summary of the data is provided.

> The first stage (age 5) is magical: we make the clouds move by walking. The second stage (age 6) is both artificialist and animistic. Clouds move because God or men make them move. During a third stage (age 7) clouds are supposed to move by themselves, but, in addition, the sun and moon, etc., also make the clouds move, not as a physical cause but through a command. . . . According to children of the fourth stage (age 8), the wind pushes the clouds. When finally the fifth stage is reached (age 9), a correct explanation is found.[1]

What can you tell from such findings?

A. The characteristics of the child's conception of physical causality vary at different ages.
B. Children score higher on a measure of physical causality as they get older.

....

A. True. This approach seems to get at the characteristics or way of thinking that children evidence at different levels as distinct from simply the number of questions they can answer on a test. In other words, it gets at the qualities of the thought processes through an analysis of the child's answers to questions as opposed to simply the quantity of correct answers he is able to give.
B. It's not a question of "higher score" so much as different kind of answer. Also, the question wasn't really designed as a measure

---

[1] Abridged from *The Child's Conception of Physical Causality* by Jean Piaget, Kegan Paul, London, 1930, pp. 61-62.

in the strict sense but as a lead question to elicit verbal responses; therefore, choice A is the better response.

Jean Piaget (b. 1896), Professor of Psychology at the University of Geneva and Director of the J. J. Rousseau Institute there, has been studying the thought processes of children—and to a lesser extent adolescents—for over fifty years. As we have seen, his approach is qualitative as distinguished from the quantitative approach of the American developmental psychologists before 1960. From the beginning of his career in Binet's laboratory at a Paris grade school, Piaget was interested not so much in how well the children scored on mental tests but in the *processes* they used in arriving at their answers—especially the incorrect answers.

How extensive and significant has his work been over the years? Your judgment about the significance of his ideas, particularly for education, will have to await the completion of this book and, hopefully, some of Piaget's books themselves. As far as the *extent* of his work is concerned, take a few seconds to scan the bibliography in the back of the book.

Would you say that his books (most of his 100 or more journal articles are not included) represent:

A. a moderate variety of studies on some interesting aspects of cognitive development.

B. extensive work on many aspects of cognitive development.

....

A. Even acknowledging that the terms "moderate" and "extensive" are relative, over twenty books on such a variety of aspects of cognitive development still seem more than a "moderate" variety of studies.

B. There is no one in the history of psychology who has studied children more extensively than Jean Piaget. He has studied the development of their basic ways of thinking as well as their concepts of number, time, space, physical causality, life, morality, etc., to say nothing of their language and perceptual development. On the basis of his extensive research, he has formulated the first major theory of cognitive development in the history of developmental psychology. He has been called "giant," "genius," and the "Freud of developmental psychology." Again, whether or not you agree with this judgment should await at least your completion of this introduction to his theory and hopefully your having read him in the "original."

If Piaget is so important, why wasn't his work accepted by American developmental psychologists for so many years—not until the early 1960s?

Consider the following summary of a typical research study conducted in the 1950s by two American psychologists.

The S's were children of preschool age. The criterion task was a simultaneous discrimination problem and the stimuli were a pair of pen-and-ink sketches of girls' faces. The design included a relevant-stimulus and an irrelevant-stimulus group of 26 S's each; another group of 18 S's received discriminative experience with the relevant-stimuli but did not receive name-learning experience.

TABLE 1
Number of Correct Responses in Thirty Transfer Trials

Age	Group R Mean	Group R SD	Group I Mean	Group I SD	Group D Mean	Group D SD
Younger	19.5	6.0	15.9	3.7	17.1	5.0
Older	24.8	6.2	22.4	5.6	19.2	4.3

The results shown in Table 1, in terms of the number of correct responses in 30 criterion task trials, demonstrated the relevant-stimulus group to be superior to the irrelevant and discrimination groups, whereas the latter two did not differ significantly.[2]

Compare this study with Piaget's summary of his "clouds" study.

Why do you think Piaget was not accepted by American psychologists for so many years?

A. His studies weren't statistically based.

B. His early work had little bearing on child development.

---

[2] K. J. Norcross and C. C. Spiker, "The Effects of Type of Stimulus Pretraining on Discrimination Performance in Preschool Children," *Child Development* 28 (1957): 79–84.

A. True. American psychologists have traditionally emphasized statistical tests of probability as *the* way of determining whether something is "true" or not. Piaget never bothered with statistics or with much quantitative analysis, for that matter; as a result, he appeared to Americans as "nonscientific," "impressionistic," etc. Also, most Americans were behaviorally oriented and did not treat with much respect Piaget's attempt to examine the child's internal thought processes.

But all of a sudden in the '60s, the psychological pendulum began to swing from a strict behaviorist approach toward a more cognitive and personalist view of the child. Americans became aware of the significant insights that Piaget had gained from his forty years of studying children through observing them and asking them questions to discover the qualities of their thinking.

By the mid-'60s scores of Piaget-based studies had been conducted and practically all papers on child development delivered at psychological conventions were either based on or at least referred to Piaget's work. A climax was reached at the 1969 American Educational Research Association convention when Piaget addressed several thousand psychologists and educational researchers. As one observer reported on his entrance into the auditorium, "It was as though Caesar was returning as a conquering hero; the air seemed to part in front of him."

B. There's really no basis for this conclusion. Even the little we've seen so far would indicate that Piaget's work has as much relevance to the development of the child as any quantitative research conducted by Americans. Choice A is appropriate.

Here is a sample of Piaget's more recent work. What do you think of it in terms of its degree of difficulty?

> Classes. Classes may be defined both by their "intension" and by the "extension." This distinction is not perfected until the stage of equilibrium reached at 9-10 years. As far as intension is concerned, we know from the Binet and Simon test on definitions that children below this age tend to give definitions by use rather than definitions by genus and differentia. As far as extension is concerned, our experiments on "all" and "some" show that younger children have an imperfect grasp of the quantitative relations involved. . . .

Definition 1. Given a family of classes, A, A' and B, such that B = A + A' and A × A' = O (A' being therefore the complement of A with respect to B, since A and A' are disjoint), the "intension" of a class is the set of properties common to the members of that class, together with the set of differences which distinguish them from another class.[3]

Would you say Piaget, at least in his more recent works, is

A. moderately easy?

B. quite difficult?

....

A. If you consider him moderately easy, I would suggest that you delve directly into Piaget himself, perhaps starting with *The Psychology of The Child* for an overview and then *The Early Growth of Logic* and *The Growth of Logical Thinking* for a more detailed analysis.

B. Most students—even psychologists—would agree that Piaget, especially in his more recent writings, is a very difficult author to read. It is particularly his use of propositional logic as a model for examining the thought processes of children and adolescents (in somewhat the same way as some learning theorists use mathematical models in their analyses of learning) that makes his recent books quite difficult to follow, unless one has a background in symbolic logic. His earlier works, on the other hand, are quite readable, for example, *The Language and Thought of the Child, Judgment and Reasoning in the Child* and *The Psychology of Intelligence.*

What about this present introduction to the thought of Piaget? First of all, its purpose is to try to make Piaget's theory understandable to teachers and teacher education students who might not have the extensive background in developmental psychology and symbolic logic needed to read Piaget in the "original." Secondly, it stresses the school years, and particularly the general qualities of child and adolescent thought that are important for a teacher to be aware of. Thirdly, it attempts to draw some preliminary applications of Piaget's thought to teaching strategies and the curriculum. Finally, you may have noticed that the approach or format is a little different from the ordinary expository text. It might be called a "discovery program" approach. On the basis

---

[3] From *The Early Growth of Logic in the Child* by Bärbel Inhelder and Jean Piaget, Harper and Row, New York, 1964, p. 7.

of the half-dozen or so "frames" you have gone through so far, what would you say your role in the book will be?

A. A receiver of information which is presented to you.

B. An active participant who will have to analyze data and derive conclusions from it.

....

A. You'll be disappointed if you want an expository type of introduction to Piaget. This is definitely not one. I would suggest that you select one of the other introductions listed in the bibliography.

B. Right. What I've tried to do in this book is replicate the approach that Piaget uses in his research. First, a Piaget-type problem is presented together with a capsule transcript or two of how some children or adolescents have solved the problem; then you are encouraged to be actively engaged and to derive an element of theory from the data. This active, discovery-oriented approach is very much in keeping with Piaget's view of learning and how knowledge is acquired. According to him, you as a learner have to manipulate the data and either form new cognitive structures or incorporate the data into your existing structures. Also, since most of the ideas will probably be rather new to you, the inductive approach—from data to conclusion, from instances to generalization—should be more effective in helping you understand the material than a more abstract, expository presentation would be; at least, that's what Piaget suggests.

Chapter 2

The
Preschool
Years

From birth until the time he enters school, the child develops an amazing number of abilities and habits. This chapter will identify only a few of the main ones, particularly those that have some relation to the abilities and operations that' develop later during the school years. The main implication to be drawn is that the elementary school pupil's thinking is not based on a vacuum but grows out of and in many respects is based on the thinking of the preschool child.

The situations or "problems" examined are adapted from several sources including *The Language and Thought of the Child, Judgment and Reasoning in the Child,* and *The Psychology of the Child.*

Observation. The following behavior is observed in two infants.

Andy, age 3 mos.   He opens and closes his fists and is seen fingering his blanket.

Bob, age 4½ mos.   He is seen to grab at almost anything that is near him: a rattle, a hanging cord, the side of the crib to move a mobile.

What ability does Bob (4½ mos.) show signs of having developed?

A. Manual movement and control.

B. Coordination of vision and manual movement.

....

A. Andy (3 mos.) already shows an ability to move and control his hands to some extent, but Bob's development is more advanced. See response B.

B. Correct. The ability to grab at things requires the coordination of the eyes and hands. This is an example of one of the early sensori-motor abilities or "schemes"—as Piaget calls them—to develop in the infant. The child spends the first year and a half or so of life in acquiring the various sensori-motor schemes, from the simpler habits as grasping to the more complicated coordinations as running and using a spoon to feed himself. Some of these identifiable sensori-motor sequences, for instance, in the above observation the coordinating of eye and hand and moving the crib to make the mobile move (using a means to an end), prefigure some of the cognitive coordinations and relationships that will develop years later.

Situation. The baby is playing with an empty milk bottle with a "funny face" painted on it. She is obviously absorbed in it and enjoying her play. She drops it and the parent takes it and puts it behind a pillow.

Connie, age 7 mos. She looks at the pillow for a moment and then looks around for something else to play with.

Donna, age 9 mos. She moves the pillow and gets the bottle behind it.

What awareness does Donna show that Connie does not?

A. The object (bottle) still exists even though hidden from view.

B. Grasping for things is the way to get them back.

....

A. Right. What Donna gives evidence of is an awareness of an object as permanent, as still existing even when out of sight. To Connie the world consists of "shifting and unsubstantial tableaux." If something goes out of her sight, it seems to her simply to be absorbed into the surrounding environment. But Donna shows that she realizes objects do not cease to exist when they are put out of her sight. This awareness—or "scheme"—of the permanent object, involving the realization that the object is conserved even though transferred in space beyond one's vision, serves as a basis for and in a sense foreshadows another type of "conservation" which, as will be shown, is extremely important for the primary grade pupil.

B. The "scheme" or sensori-motor ability of grasping in order to get things was in evidence even in Bob (4½ mos.) in the last situation. Donna's awareness is more advanced. Check again on her reaction and see if you don't agree with A.

Observations. The following observations were made by parents.

Earl, age 1 yr., 10 mos. He picks up a stick and makes believe it is a gun.

Frank, age 1 yr., 10 mos. He says "buh-un" (button) as he fingers the button on his mother's dress.

What seems to be common to these two incidents?

A. Both Earl and Frank show evidence of an ability to let something stand for or represent something else.

B. Earl and Frank give evidence of a perceptual alertness not found at previous levels.

....

A. This definitely seems to be what is at work in these two instances, namely, the ability to let an object or a series of sounds serve as a sign of something else. Whether the "sign" takes the form of language or symbolic play, the underlying ability or function seems to be the same, i.e., the ability to let one thing stand for another. Piaget terms this ability the "symbolic function." It is the basis for one of the great learnings in the life of the child—the learning of a language—which, in turn, is fundamental to much of the learning and behavior that will be acquired later on. The appearance of the symbolic function, then, is one of the great milestones in the development of the child.

B. First of all, it is much more than perceptual alertness that is involved here. Second, perceptual abilities develop to a significant degree quite a bit earlier, i.e., by the second half of the first year. Response A explains what is happening in these two incidents.

Problem. The child is asked what the following sentence means:

"Small people may be of great worth."

Gail, age 6. "It means that they may get bigger later on."

It is quite obvious that Gail did not understand the meaning of the word "worth." What do you think is at work in her interpretation of the sentence?

A. She understood most of it and then made up a meaning to fill in for the part she didn't understand.

B. She said whatever came to her mind whether it had any relation to the sentence or not.

....

A. This is exactly what she seems to have done. She got a general idea of the sentence on the basis of the words she was familiar with and then simply filled in for the word she didn't know with some idea that seemed to fit. In other words, the child lets the difficult word(s) go, forms a general meaning out of the familiar words, and then interprets the words she doesn't understand in terms of that general meaning. To the child, this is perfectly satisfactory. She is interested in the whole (the general idea), not in analyzing each and every part (specific words). Piaget terms this quality of the child's thinking "syncretism"—from the Greek "to combine or fuse together." It lasts until the child enters school and even a short time after.

B. It might have seemed like this, but she really comprehended most of the sentence. What she stated was for the most part related to the full meaning; she just didn't grasp all of it. A is the correct explanation.

Problem. The child is asked: "Why does the sun stay up?"

Hal, age 6. "Because it's bright."

Ira, age 7. "Because it's daytime."

What do you notice about the reasons that these children give?

A. The "reasons" show lack of information more than an inability to give a real reason.

B. The "reasons" are other related facts that are offered to explain the phenomenon of the sun staying up.

....

A. Granted the children don't possess the required information, but if you were to try a similar experiment with some six-year-olds, you would find that they give "reasons" right away. On the other hand, nine-year-olds, for example, first tend to say "I don't know," but after some thought, might give an explanation that uses the idea of "no force of gravity." This indicates that the older children appreciate what real reasons entail and often hesitate because they feel they don't have the required information. But younger children give their "reasons" right away and they are quite certain of them—even though they are not genuine reasons. All of this leads to the conclusion that younger children simply cannot yet give a logical reason for something. See if B doesn't follow more from the data.

B. Agreed. The children use one fact to support another fact. It's a kind of syncretism of reasoning in that two facts are combined or "fused together" with the intention that one fact explain the other. This type of reasoning moves from particular to particular without any awareness of logical necessity. It isn't inductive (particular to general) or deductive (general to particular). Piaget termed it "trans-ductive," i.e., it simply juxtaposes two particular facts with one sup-posedly explaining the other. It is rather obvious, therefore, that there is no real logical reasoning before age seven or eight.

Summary. Piaget distinguishes three stages of development during the first six years or so of life: sensori-motor, symbolic thought, and intuitive thought. The stages with some of their main characteristics plus average ages are summarized below.

Sensori-motor (0 to 2)

Characterized by the development of the sensori-motor reflexes and actions, eye-hand coordination, means-ends relations, and the awareness of the permanent object

Symbolic thought (2 to 4)

Characterized by the development of the symbolic function evidenced in language and symbolic play

Intuitive thought (4 to 7)

Characterized by—among other things—syncretism (fusing together) in understanding and by transductive reasoning (one fact "explains" another)

Chapter 3

The Elementary School Pupil

About the time the child enters elementary school, he makes some dramatic advances in his thinking ability. It is these advances that we now want to consider as we examine such questions as: How do the elementary school child's thought processes differ from those of the preschool child's? What intellectual operations can he now perform? What are some of the specific characteristics of his thought processes? Are they the same as or different from those of the adolescent (or adult)?

As we did in the previous chapter on the preschool child, we will analyze some problems and experiments that will illustrate the qualities of the thinking of the elementary school pupil. The problems have been taken mainly from Piaget's writings on number and physical causality; some of them are summarized in *The Psychology of the Child*.

The main types of intellectual operations that the elementary school child can perform can be derived from the following several experiments.

Problem #1. Twenty wooden beads, 16 brown and 4 white, are presented to the child with the question: Are there more brown beads or wooden beads? ● ● ● ● ● ● ● ● ● ● ● ● ● ● ● ● o o o o

15

Ann, age 5. "There are more brown beads."

Bill, age 7. "There are more wooden beads than brown beads."

What can we derive from this simple example?

A. Bill was able to group the brown and white beads together into the class "wooden beads."

B. Ann simply did not understand the question.

C. Bill perceived the obvious fact that there are more wooden beads.

....

A. To answer the question correctly some grouping or manipulation of objects perceived is necessary, viz., the grouping of two types, brown and white, into one class—wooden. You are correct.

B. It is more probable that she was unable to perform the internal operation necessary to answer correctly; therefore, this is not the best response.

C. There's more to it than this. It might seem obvious to us, but an operation more complex than perception, namely, that of grouping, is necessary for the solution. Answer A is a better explanation.

Another similar problem is as follows:

Problem #2. "Are there more boys or children in your class?"

Cora, age 5. "There are more boys than girls."

Dawn, age 6. "There are more children; there are both boys and girls."

What was Dawn able to do that Cora was not?

A. Distinguish between boys and girls.

B. Combine parts into a whole.

C. Define "children."

....

A. Even younger children know the difference between boys and girls. However, when they are called on to combine them they have trouble. Check choices B and C.

B. Correct. The problem called for combining or grouping boys and girls into a whole, i.e., children.

C. There's more to answering the problem than simply defining terms;
   grouping is what is called for, as explained in B.

Now consider another simple experiment.

Problem #3. Ten wooden rods of varying length (1cm. to 10cm.) are
mixed and presented to the child with the instructions: put them in
order from the smallest to the largest.

Eric, age 6. He puts 3cm. next to 8cm., 2cm. next to 7cm., 10cm.
next to 4cm., 6cm. next to 1cm., 5cm. next to 9 cm.

Fred, age 6. He starts with 1cm., puts 2cm. next, 3cm. next, etc.,
in order from shortest to longest.

What can we derive from this example?

A. Eric did not understand the directions.

B. Fred perceived the rods as small and large.

C. Fred grouped the rods according to an order (of size).

....

A. The directions were quite clear and simple. He was more probably
   unable to form an adequate concept of "smallest" and "largest." See
   the other responses.

B. *Eric* also perceived the rods as small and large; in fact, this was the
   root of his inability to solve the problem correctly. There is a better
   answer to the question.

C. Correct. This grouping into an order or series which requires first
   distinguishing between smaller and larger and then relating all of
   the rods into a series from smallest to largest is what is required
   to solve the problem.

Another similar experiment is as follows:

Problem # 4. A set of eight graduated slats is arranged in the form of a staircase; seven other slats whose sizes are intermediate to those in the first set are presented to the child with the instructions: insert or put these into the staircase so that it makes a larger staircase.

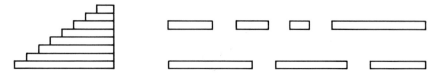

Gwen, age 5. She builds another staircase next to the first.

Herb, age 6. He inserts the slats into the staircase but with no real plan or order.

Ida, age 8. She inserts the second set of slats into the first in the proper order.

What was Ida (8) able to do that Gwen and Herb were not?

A. Compose the relations "greater than" and "less than."

B. Build an ordered staircase with different sized slats.

....

A. This is exactly what was required to solve the problem. The child had to, for instance, grasp that the longest of the second set is less than the bottom slat of the staircase but greater than the one next to the bottom.

B. Even the preschool child (e.g., Gwen) can build a staircase; it takes more than this to solve the problem, namely, relating all of the slats into an order. Response A is correct.

Now to consolidate what we have derived from these experiments. The specific type of grouping of objects illustrated in Problems 1 and 2 (the beads and the children) is that of:

A. classifying: grouping objects similar in some way into a class.

B. perceiving: synthesizing sensations into an awareness of an object.

C. ordering: grouping objects into an order from least to greatest.

....

A. Correct. The subjects had to grasp the common element and put parts into a whole, in a word, classify. This is one of the two main types of grouping that the elementary school child can perform.

B. Perception requires "grouping" or synthesizing sensations into the perception of an object. But this is achieved 1) on the level of the internal senses rather than that of thought and 2) at a much earlier age. Consequently, perception is not the type of grouping illustrated in these problems.

C. Ordering wasn't really exemplified in the beads or the children problems. Recall, for instance, that the beads problem called for the child to group the brown and white beads into wooden beads.

The manipulation or grouping of objects exemplified in Problems 3 and 4 (the rods and the staircase) is that of:

A. ordering: grouping objects into an order from least to greatest (or vice versa).

B. discriminating: perceiving the differences among objects.

C. classifying: grouping objects similar in some way into a class.

....

A. Correct. The child had to put the objects into an order or relate them into a series. This ordering or putting into some relation is the other main type of grouping possible for the elementary child. Piaget refers to it as "seriation." Although the examples given involve an ordering according to "greater than," there are other types of orders or series, viz., "before and after" in time or space.

B. Discriminating is called for, but it was also necessary for the younger child in Problem 3 when he juxtaposed a short and a long rod or in Problem 4 when he constructed a second staircase; therefore, it cannot be the essential factor at work here. Recall that the rods and the staircase problems called for an ordering of the objects involved. Again, what type of grouping did these problems require?

C. The grouping in the rods and the staircase problems is of another type than classifying. There is not a common element or parts of a whole involved here, but an order or series. Choice A is the best response.

We have seen that those who solved Problems 1 through 4 successfully, grouped or manipulated the objects in some way. Was this grouping of objects mainly internal or external?

A. Internal—in their minds.

B. External—overt.

....

A. Correct. Bill (7) solved the beads problem, i.e., grouped brown and white beads into wooden beads without any overt manipulation; likewise for Dawn (6) in the children problem. In the rods and slats problems, Fred (6) and Ida (8) definitely seem to have done the ordering in their minds before they actually put the objects in order externally.

B. How about Bill? Did he group the beads externally in answering the question? No. Similarly for Dawn in the children problem. Fred and Ida did manipulate the rods and the slats overtly, but they couldn't have done it so quickly—and correctly—without figuring the order out in their minds first. Recall what took place in Problems 1 through 4 and see if you don't agree with choice A.

Now let's examine some further characteristics of the elementary school child's way of thinking by analyzing some additional experiments and seeing what elements of theory we can derive from them. One of the most famous of Piaget's experiments is the following.

Problem #5. Two equal cylinders are filled with water; the experimenter makes sure the subject is satisfied that they are equal (1). The water from one is then poured into a flat round container (2), and the question is presented: Which has more or are they equal?

(1)   (2)

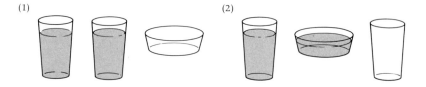

Jane, age 5. "This one [cylinder] has more. It's higher."
Ken, age 6. "This one [flat container]." Why? "Because it's bigger [gesturing width with both hands]."

Lois, age 7. "They're equal."

Milo, age 8. "They're the same; you poured all the water into the flat dish."

What have Lois and Milo been able to do that Jane and Ken couldn't seem to do?

A. Form perceptions of actions.

B. Take into account both shape and quantity of something.

C. Judge whether or not two quantities are equal.

....

A. It's much more than a question of just perceiving objects or actions. Jane (5) and Ken (6) perceive the action, but they can't perform the mental operation necessary to solve the problem. The question is what this required mental operation is.

B. Correct. This taking into account two aspects of something—in this case water—seems to be the basic characteristic of the thinking of Lois (7) and Milo (8) which allowed them to solve the problem successfully. They are able to *coordinate* shape and quantity, consider them both at once, and hence *conserve* the aspect of quantity even though the shape changes.

C. It takes more than this. When the experimenter started out, he asked Jane (5) and Ken (6) if the water in the two cylinders was equal, and they were able to tell him whether it was or not. To realize whether it is equal when the water from one cylinder has been poured into a flat container requires something else.

Here is another experiment that demonstrates the same characteristic of the child's thinking.

Problem #6. Six coins of the same denomination are laid out one inch apart; six more coins of the same size are laid out below each of the first six (1). The experimenter makes sure the child is satisfied that the number of coins in each row is equal. Then he spreads the first set so that they are four inches apart (2). The question is asked: Are there more here (top) or here (bottom) or are they equal?

(1) o o o o o o   (2) o   o o o o o   o
      o o o o o o   o o o o o o o

Nan, age 5. "There are more here [top]."

Otto, age 7. "They're equal. You just moved them."

What can we derive from this experiment?

A. Otto was able to conserve quantity.

B. Otto was able to count more accurately than Nan.

....

A. Correct. What the child must do to solve this problem is to conserve the aspect of quantity—in this case discontinuous quantity—even though position or arrangement is changed. Again, the two aspects of something, in this instance quantity and arrangement, must be taken into account at the same time and coordinated with each other. This is basically what is involved in forming the concept of number, realizing that the number of things remains the same even though their arrangement is changed.

B. Nan, a typical preschool child, can count quite well. However, problems which require mental operations give her trouble. Choice A explains the operation that was required to solve the problem.

Considering both the problems of the cylinders and the coins, what would you say was the root of the difficulty experienced by Jane (5), Ken (6), and Nan (5) in their inability to solve the problems?

A. Their thinking was centered on only one aspect of the object.

B. They were too impulsive in their thinking.

....

A. This definitely seems to be the root of their problem. Those who solved the problems successfully (Lois, 7; Milo, 8; and Otto, 7) were able to "decenter" their thinking and concentrate on two aspects at once. Actually, this decentering and the coordination of aspects are two sides of the same coin: decentering is the negative side and coordination, the positive side. In order to conserve one aspect of something (e.g., quantity) through a transformation of another aspect (e.g., shape or arrangement), the child must be able to both (1) decenter his thinking—take into account both aspects at once—and then (2) coordinate the two aspects and realize how they are related—that changing one does not change the other.

B. They are quite certain that what they think to be true is actually true, and they frequently try to answer the problem to the best of their ability. Therefore, impulsiveness is not their problem.

A very important—Piaget considers it most important—characteristic of the elementary school child's thought is illustrated in the next few problems.

Problem #7. What is 12 + 6? How can you get 12 again?

Peg, age 5. "I don't know."
Ray, age 7. "12 + 6 = 18; 18 − 6 = 12."

What was Ray able to do that Peg was not?

A. Use the operation of addition to solve the problem.
B. Grasp that one operation can be cancelled out by an inverse operation.
C. Grasp that one variable can compensate for another variable.

....

A. Ray was able to add (also subtract), true; but this is only part of the story. Read the problem again and see if you can't discern another characteristic of his thought process.

B. Correct. The problem calls for the ability to grasp that one operation, e.g., addition, can be negated or cancelled out by an inverse or complementary operation, viz., subtraction.

C. This is not quite what is at work here. It is not a question of variables but of operations reversing one another.

What would you say is at work in the solving of this next problem?

Problem #8. The child is given a balance with a 3 oz. weight on either platform (1) and other weights of different sizes. When a 1 oz. weight is added to one side (2), the question is posed: Can you make it even again?

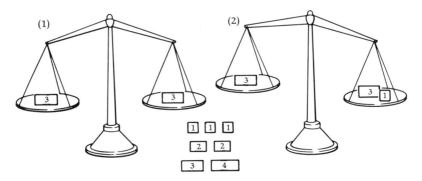

Sue, age 5. "You could put one on the other side [placing a 2 oz. weight]. That doesn't work; maybe there's too much weight."

Toni, age 7. "You have to put the same weight on each side [putting a 1 oz. weight on the other side]. There, it's equal again."

What was Toni able to do that Sue seemed unable to?

A. Revert back to the starting point after an operation had been performed.

B. Increase the amount of weight on the imbalanced side.

....

A. This is exactly what Toni (7) was able to do: to return to the starting point of the problem after an operation had changed the situation. You will notice that she did it by performing a complementary operation, i.e., adding an equal weight to the other side. This is essentially the same as what Ray (7) did in the last problem: reverse an operation and come back to the point of departure or to equilibrium. Piaget termed this characteristic of the thought processes of the elementary school child *reversibility.*

B. Toni did this all right, but so did Sue—and Sue was unable to solve the problem. There is obviously more to the problem than simply adding weight to the other side of the balance. Reread the problem and see if you agree with A.

We can actually distinguish two types of reversibility. Recall the conservation of continuous quantity (water) problem.

(1)   (2)

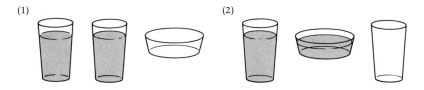

When a child who has solved the problem correctly is asked why the amounts are equal, he might answer something like:

"You only poured it; you didn't take any away"; or
"You can put the water back in the glass where it was before"; or
"It's spread out but the glass is higher, so it's the same amount."

The first of these reasons simply states the *identity* of the water; it's the same, nothing has been added or taken away. But the other two reasons refer to a change, a transformation, particularly that of reversibility.

Which would you say is involved more in the statement: "You can put the water back"?

A. Cancelling out the original action (of pouring).

B. Compensating or making up for the original action.

....

A. Agreed. The child saw that the quantity was the same for the reason that if you did the opposite or inverse operation you would end up with the same amount that you started with. Piaget calls this "reversibility by inversion." Another example is reversing by subtraction which is the inverse of addition (cf. Problem 7).

B. Close but not exactly right. In putting the water back, the child is not really compensating for an action but is doing what is explained in A.

What type of reversibility is represented by the statement: "The water is spread out more but the glass is higher; so it's the same amount"?

A. Cancelling out the original action of pouring.

B. Compensating or making up for the original action.

....

A. Ask yourself what is at work here: is it cancelling out through the inverse operation or is it making up for the fact that the water is spread out by the fact that the other water is in a taller container?

B. Right. The fact that the glass is taller makes up for or compensates for the fact that the other container is much wider. Piaget terms this use of compensation in the thinking of the child "reversibility by reciprocal relationship" or simply "reciprocity." Recall the example of the balance (Problem 8) in which the child rebalanced the scale by putting an equal weight on the other side. This is another example of reversibility by compensation or reciprocity, i.e., making up for one force or action by another (compensating) force or action.

For one final characteristic of the elementary pupil's thinking let's analyze the following question and responses.

Problem #9. There are three girls: Mary, Jennie and Sally. Mary is lighter (in complexion) than Sally; Mary is darker than Jennie. Who is darkest of all?

Una, age 7. "The middle one; I couldn't follow."

Vera, age 9. "Jennie." Why? "Well, the first two are light and Jennie is dark."

Win, age 10. "Mary; no, Sally." Why? "I'm not sure; I can never figure those out."

What can we tell about the thinking of the elementary school child from the above responses?

A. Children at these ages can't handle the concepts of "lighter—darker," "greater—less," etc.

B. Children at this age can't handle problems presented on a purely verbal level.

....

A. Actually children at these ages *can* understand the concepts of "lighter," "greater," etc. What is necessary for them to form these concepts is to be able to relate things in an order, which—as we have seen—they can do. Their problem here is not one of ordering but of thinking on a verbal level. See B for an explanation.

B. True. If they had Mary, Sally and Jennie in front of them or if they had seen them previously, they would be able to answer the question correctly, but on a purely verbal or abstract level they are unable to do so.

On the basis of the experiments and transcripts that we have analyzed so far, which description do you think best characterizes the thought processes of the elementary school child?

A. Concrete operations.

B. Abstract thinking.

C. Perceptual level.

....

A. Agreed. Their thinking is dependent on concrete, perceptible data, and it also involves genuine operations or internal manipulations of the data. For these reasons, Piaget termed the thinking of children at this stage "concrete operational thought."

B. Go back to the last problem (Mary-Jennie-Sally) and see whether you really think the children are capable of purely abstract thought. You might also recall the other problems and transcripts; none of them provided any evidence of abstract thinking on this age level. Internal, yes; abstract, no.

C. The thinking of elementary school children is dependent upon the objects they perceive, true. But they can do more than perceive at this level. In fact, their thinking is markedly different and much more advanced than that of the mainly perceptual preschool level. See choice A.

What type of reasoning would you judge is more in keeping with this concrete operational thinking that we have been analyzing?

A. Inductive: deriving generalizations from particular instances.

B. Deductive: deriving implied conclusions from generalizations.

....

A. Agreed. In inductive thinking we start with concrete objects or specific instances and derive a generalization from them. The elementary school child can grasp principles and relationships if he can induce them from specific examples or instances. In a word, his reasoning is mainly inductive.

B. Although the elementary school child can make simple applications or deductions from generalizations that he has already induced, he can't really start with a verbal generalization and then deduce further conclusions from it. Choice A is the better answer.

From the sample transcripts we have seen, at what age does a child begin to be capable of concrete operational thinking?

A. Seven.

B. About six or seven.

....

A. Seven seems to be a key age for the development of operational thinking, but many children achieve this stage at age six, a few even at five, and some not until eight. You can't really pinpoint it to one age. B is a more flexible answer.

B. Most children are able to do operational thinking at age six or seven. However, there will be a few five-year-olds who have already reached this stage; and then there will be a few who will not arrive at operational thought until eight. In his research, Piaget found that there is fairly wide individual variation in the transition from one stage to another. But on the average, children advance to the stage of concrete operations at about six or seven. Their concrete thinking continues to develop and reaches a state of relative maturity or "equilibrium" at about 9 or 10. Then, at 11 or 12, they advance to the next major stage of thought—which we will analyze in the following chapter.

Review. We have identified several operations and characteristics of the thought processes of elementary school children through our analysis of some simple experiments. To review, the following is a list of these operations and the qualities of the thought processes of the concrete operational child (ages 6 or 7 to ages 11 or 12):

Operations: internal manipulation or grouping of objects perceived

Classifying: grouping objects into a class

Ordering: relating objects in an order or series

Characteristics of thought processes

Internal: the groupings go on in the child's mind: overt action, although frequently involved, is not absolutely necessary

Concrete: the child manipulates or groups what he has perceived; his thinking is dependent on the concrete, real world

Decentralization of thought: rather than center on only one aspect, the child is able to concentrate on two aspects of something at the same time

Coordination of aspects: the child is able to take into account two aspects of something, e.g., shape and quantity, and coordinate them with each other

Reversibility: the child is able to revert back to the starting point in a problem, to cancel out the effect of one operation through the inverse operation (Inversion) or to compensate for the effect of one action through a reciprocal action (Reciprocity)

Type of reasoning

Inductive: the child derives generalizations from concrete instances

Chapter 4

The
Junior
and
Senior
High
Student

In contrast to the level of thinking proper to the elementary school child, let's now examine some of the striking advances in intellectual activity made by the junior and senior high student. In many cases, we will try something different from the last chapter. For example, rather than provide two experiments for each quality of the thought processes, we will try to analyze each experiment more fully, looking for one or more points of Piaget's theory in each.[1]

An experiment designed to illustrate two important aspects of preadolescent and adolescent thinking is the following.

Problem #1. A small "billiard table" and a cue stick are provided for the subject with the following instructions: standing only at the corner indicated, hit the cue ball so that it bounces off the opposite side and hits the target (to be placed successively in the positions indicated). He is then asked to comment on the way the ball bounces off the opposite side, i.e., what can be said about the angle at which it rebounds.

---

[1] Problems have been taken either directly or adapted from *The Growth of Logical Thinking From Childhood to Adolescence* by Bärbel Inhelder and Jean Piaget, Basic Books, Inc., Publishers, New York, 1958.

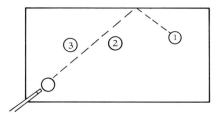

Abe, age 9. Several trials. "The more you turn the cue this way [to the right] the more the ball will bounce off like that [increasingly obtuse angle]. If you hit it straight, it will come right back."

Beth, age 15. "I think it comes off at a right angle." Several trials. "No. The rebound depends on the angle of the cue stick." Another trial. "If you imagine a perpendicular line, then the angle formed by the stick and the angle of the rebound are equal."

What is the difference in approach to the problem between the two subjects?

A. Abe was unable to derive any conclusion from his trials.

B. Beth started thinking in terms of possibilities; whereas, Abe based his conclusion simply on his observations.

....

A. Actually, Abe was able to induce an order or relationship among the several inclinations of the cue stick and among the several angles of rebound; he was also able to establish a correspondence between the two series of angles. So he really did derive something from his trials. See answer B.

B. Correct. This ability to start with one or more possibilities is one of the major advances of the high school student over the elementary pupil. The latter is still limited by the real, observable, concrete world; whereas the former can begin his solving of problems by thinking first of hypotheses or possibilities and then proceeding to examine them systematically. This hypothetico-deductive thinking, as Piaget calls it, involves the subordination of reality to possibility, a new relationship which is the inverse of the domination of thought by reality characteristic of the earlier stage.

There is another difference between the approaches of the two subjects. Can you discern it?

A. Abe tried to show why his conclusion was necessary, not just something constant.

B. Beth tried to explain her conclusion by giving a reason or demonstration for it.

....

A. Not really. You may have thought that his hitting the ball straight was an attempt to prove the order or relationship he discovered, but this was just the "outer limit" of the series. Actually, his statement or conclusion is based on constancy; he shows no concern for establishing necessity.

B. Correct. In fact, this concern for explanation and providing a reason is one of the main things that differentiates the high school student from the elementary pupil. His need for proving his statements in terms of necessity is a definite advance over the younger student's practice of stating generalizations or relationships simply in terms of constancy.

Try another, somewhat involved problem which is one of the best for illustrating another very important characteristic of the secondary student's thought.

Problem #2. The subject is provided with four bottles of transparent, odorless liquids: 1) water, 2) oxygenated water, 3) diluted sulphuric acid, and 4) thiosulphate, plus a smaller bottle with a dropper containing 5) potassium iodide.

The experiment is based on the fact that oxygenated water (2) oxidizes potassium iodide (5) in an acid medium (3). Thus the mixture of 2, 3, and 5 will produce a yellow color. The water (1) is neutral, but the thiosulphate (4) acts as a bleaching agent. The subject is told that some combination that includes the liquid in the smaller bottle (5) will result in a yellow color. The task is to find that combination. (It will be helpful to keep in mind that 2, 3, and 5 produce yellow; but the main thing to look for is the way in which the subjects combine the various liquids.)

Carl, age 9.   He mixes 5 with 1, 5 with 2, 5 with 3, and 5 with 4. "Nothing happens." Are there other ways to mix them? "Perhaps all together." He mixes 1 and 2, then adds a drop or two of 5, adds 3—"It's starting to turn yellow!"—and finally pours some of 4 in. "It's gone away."

Doris, age 13.   She tries 1 and 5, 2 and 5, 3 and 5, 4 and 5 with no result. "I guess you have to mix them." She tries 1, 2, and 5; 1, 3, and 5; 1, 4, and 5; 2, 3, and 5. "There it is!" Are there any other ways? "I'll see." She mixes 2, 4, and 5; and then 3, 4, and 5. "No." Are there any other combinations? "By fours." She proceeds to combine 1, 2, 3, and 5. "There's yellow again. This [1] is probably water since it doesn't make any difference [from 2, 3, and 5]." She continues with other combinations—1, 3, 4, and 5; 2, 3, 4, and 5; and finally 1, 2, 3, 4, and 5—with no success. "No, somehow it's only the second and third combined with the smaller bottle—or the first, second and third—that make yellow."

Which of the following statements *best* represents what Doris was able to do that Carl wasn't?

A. Doris used more combinations than Carl.

B. Doris used a more systematic approach than Carl, i.e., all possible combinations.

....

A. It's true that Doris used more combinations, but this wasn't the key to her success. Someone else could use a few more than the five combinations Carl used and still not solve the problem. See choice B for the correct answer.

B. This very systematic approach does seem to be the key to the solution. Doris used all of the possible combinations (fourteen); whereas, Carl simply combined all of the elements by the smaller bottle (5) at first, and then all of the elements together. The latter is a very limited and elementary type of combination. The successful approach used by Doris involved a complete combinatorial system, i.e., a structured whole of all possible combinations.

This experiment exemplifies the adolescent's ability to think of all possible combinations of elements or objects; he can also construct a combinatorial system of variables, ideas, or propositions.

The following experiment will illustrate several aspects of a combinatorial system of propositions.

Problem #3. The subject is given two dice and told to throw them onto a table several times and keep track of the results. The inner portion of the table is red metal, while the outer portion is white wood. Opposite the "1" on one die a magnet is imbedded.

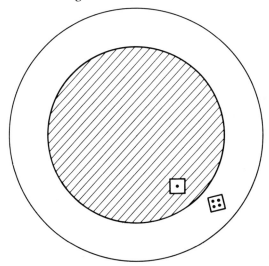

Ed, age 14.   "The 'one' shows more than any other." Why should that be? "Maybe there's a weight in one of them."

1 { More tries. "It's not a weight because 'one' doesn't always show." How can you prove that? "Well, there's either a weight in one die that always makes it come up 'one', or if it doesn't always come up 'one' there's no weight."

2 { "Let's see, it has to be either the dice or the table that causes it, or maybe both." More tries.

3 { "When the 'one' comes up it's always on the red, so it's both the dice and the middle part [of the table] that have something to do with it."

4 { "It's probably a magnet because if there's a magnet on one of them it will land the same way on the metal center part."

5 { What is the real cause? "It's both. The magnet causes the die to land with 'one' up and the die shows 'one' because it lands on the metal. It's the same thing."

After Ed induced the fact that "one" occurs more often than any other number, what is the most notable characteristic of his approach to a solution?

A. A systematic approach that sets up various hypotheses in terms of possible combinations of ideas and causes.

B. A trial and error approach in which one attempt toward a solution is made and then another.

....

A. Agreed. He combined various ideas and hypotheses into several statements containing such connectives as "both-and," "either-or," "if-then," etc. These statements represent operations that are distinctive of an adolescent's rather than a child's thinking, operations that are propositional rather than concrete.

'B. Although he did roll the dice quite a few times (trials) and did test out a second hypothesis after the first one failed, his approach could hardly be characterized by "trial and error"—which is the ordinary approach used by much younger children. Reread the transcript and see if you don't agree with A.

_____

Can you identify the "propositional combinations" used by Ed in his approach to a solution? Simply match the sections in the transcript with the proper combination.

Sections in transcript   *Combinations*

1   ____"both-and" (conjunction)

2   ____"if-then" (implication)

3   ____"either-or, or both" (disjunction)

4   ____"either-or" (mutual exclusion)

5   ____"the same as" (equivalence)

....

In Section 1 of the transcript, Ed excluded weight as a possibility and used an "either-or" approach (mutual exclusion) to prove it.

In Section 2 he combined the possibilities in what is termed a "disjunctive" way: either the dice or the table or both.

In Section 3 he joined dice and the middle part of the table together (conjunction) as a "joint possibility."

In Section 4 he states that a magnet implies or is connected in a causal way with landing the same way on the metal part. Although he doesn't use the word "then," an "if-then" type of thinking is certainly present.

Finally in Section 5 he connects two statements in a relation of equivalence, viz., that the magnet causing the "one" to show and the "one" showing when landing on the metal are for all practical purposes the same.

There are other ways of combining ideas or statements into propositions, e.g., independence of one from the other, complete affirmation or relationship of all possible combinations, plus others that are mainly the opposites of those mentioned above (e.g., incompatibility, nonimplication, contradiction, etc.). But this sample will suffice for an initial idea of the propositional operations (sixteen in all) which, when taken together, form a complete combinatorial system or "structured whole" of possibilities.

Another experiment which illustrates an important characteristic of the high school student's thinking is that of the pendulum.

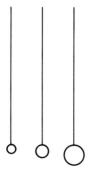 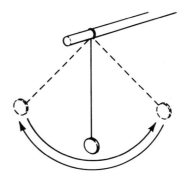

Problem #4. Three pendula of the same length but with different weights are presented to the subject (18" pieces of string with a dime, quarter and half-dollar are convenient) with the question: What determines the frequency of oscillation or how many swings a pendulum makes in a certain period of time? The subject is told that it might be the length of the string (full, ⅔, and ⅓ length are indicated), the weight (heavy, medium, light), the height of the drop, or the force of the push. The experimenter does not demonstrate these possibilities but simply gives the pendula to the subject and observes how he figures out the solution.

Fay, age 8.   She tries swinging one string at several lengths. "The higher up it is (shorter) the faster it goes." Then she tries the different weights, all at full length. "The big one goes faster; this one (dime) goes slower."

Gil, age 12.   "I think it's the length. Let's see." He uses the string with the dime and varies the length. "It goes slower when you lengthen it and faster when it's short." Is that all? "Maybe the weight does something." He then takes the quarter and lengthens and shortens the string; then the dime, doing the same. "It goes faster higher up (short); it's the string."

Hope, age 15.   She thinks for a moment. She then swings the half-dollar at full length and short length, then the quarter at full and short length, and finally the dime in the same way. She concludes: "It's the length of the string that makes it go faster or slower; the weight doesn't make any difference."

What can be derived concerning the type of thinking evidenced in these transcripts?

A. Fay (8) separates the variables and proceeds systematically.

B. Gil (12) thinks in terms of "all other things being equal."

C. Hope (15) thinks of the several possibilities and is able to control variables.

....

A. Not really. She may consider one factor at a time, but she proceeds on a concrete, trial and error basis. It's actually her lack of system that gets her into trouble. Read through the other choices.

B. He considers one factor at a time and appears to separate the variables in his mind, but he can't seem to control the variables by considering "all other things being equal." Try another answer.

C. Right. She first thinks of the most promising possibilities and then proceeds systematically, isolating one factor and controlling the other. She is the one who operates on a basis of "other things being equal."

Holding one factor constant while examining the effect of varying another factor is the key to the solution of the problem. What pattern does Hope use that illustrates this?

A. She compares long-heavy with short-heavy to see the effect on oscillation.

B. She compares long-light with short-heavy figuring that length and weight are the key factors.

....

A. Right. In this way weight is controlled, and the subject studies the effect of length on the frequency of oscillation. Similarly, she seems to compare the long-heavy with the long-light to study the effect of weight while holding length constant.

B. If the subject uses this approach, she could conclude that either increased length *or* increased weight makes the pendulum go faster. She must control one variable in order to solve the problem. Choice A explains the pattern Hope uses.

It was mentioned above that Hope first thinks of several possibilities and then proceeds systematically to examine the two most probable ones. Given below is part of a series of combinations of weights and lengths with one of the variables controlled. Which of the choices (A, B, or C) completes the series?

light–long   —   fast or slow

light–short   —   faster or slower

medium–long   —   fast or slow

A. heavy–long   —   faster or slower
B. medium–short   —   faster or slower
C. heavy–short   —   faster or slower

....

A. This choice wouldn't control weight—which is what is intended in the series.

B. Correct. This completes the series of possibilities intended to control weight while examining length.

C. This combination wouldn't control weight *or* length. Reread the series
   to determine which choice is the correct completion.

So far we have identified several of the main characteristics of the
thinking of the high school student: hypothetico-deductive thinking,
concern for proof or reasons for statements, thinking in terms of all
possible combinations of elements and ideas, and the ability to isolate
and control variables. There are other characteristics of the adolescent's
thinking that also represent advances over the elementary school child.
Let's examine some further experiments and try to identify them.

Problem #5. The subject is shown a wooden ball, a cork, a nail, and
a stone and is asked whether or not they will float on water and why.

Ivan, age 6. "The ball stays on top; it's wood; it's light. The nail goes
down; it's iron; it's heavy."

Joe, age 9. "The ball and the cork stay up because they are quite light."
How about the nail and the stone? "They go to the bottom because
they're too heavy. The wood and the cork are lighter than they are."

Karen, age 12. She classifies the objects that float or sink according
to whether they are "lighter or heavier than water." What do you mean?
"You would have to have much more water than metal to make up
the same weight."

Lew, age 15. He classifies correctly the objects that float and sink. Why
do these float and the others sink? "Taking the same volume, the water
is lighter than the stone, but the wood is lighter than an equal amount
of water." Can you demonstrate this? "I could take a wooden cube and
a plastic cube filled with water and weigh them. Then you could see
by the difference in weight whether an object is lighter or heavier than
water."

These sample transcripts show the gradual progression of the thought
processes, i.e., from the absolute type of thinking (light, heavy) of the
preoperational child (Ivan) to the ability to think in relative terms that

develops in the concrete operational stage (Joe); from simple ordering (Joe) to the more difficult comparison between water and metal (Karen). The progression continues through the significant advances evidenced in Lew's responses. What was Lew able to do that the younger subjects were not?

A. Form an abstract concept.

B. Form a true relationship.

....

A. Agreed. Have you ever seen "an equal amount of water" or a displaced quantity of water? It is not a perceivable but a purely abstract entity. This ability to form pure abstract ideas, those which have no direct basis in the perceivable world, is one of the distinct advances of the adolescent over the concrete thinker.

B. Actually, even concrete operational children (e.g., Joe) can think in terms of relationship. Also, Karen, who is at the transition point between concrete and a higher level of thinking, certainly thinks in terms of relationships, i.e., "lighter or heavier than water." A is the more appropriate response.

_____

Although Lew does not use the exact word, what he has grasped is the concept of relative density, e.g., "the wood is lighter (weight) than an equal amount (volume) of water." Density is defined as weight per unit of volume or, more exactly, the ratio of mass to volume.

What is essentially involved in this concept of density?

A. Combining two concepts to form a more abstract concept.

B. Comparing two objects so as to determine their relationship.

....

A. Agreed. Density is a "second order" concept, i.e., composed of two other previously formed concepts—in this case, weight and volume. While ordinary "first order" concepts are induced or abstracted from concrete instances, "second order" concepts are derived from two or more regular concepts. They are, therefore, even further removed from the concrete and even more abstract than regular concepts. It is clear from the transcripts that the ability to form this more abstract "second order" concept is only found on the high school level.

B. As was stated before, even a child at the concrete operational stage, such as Joe, is capable of comparing objects and determining their relationship. The concept of density involves a more abstract process.

You may recall another experiment that is relevant here.

Problem #6. There are three girls: Mary, Jennie, and Sally. Mary is lighter than Sally; Mary is darker than Jennie. Who is darkest of all?

Milo, age 9. "Jennie." Why? "Well, the first two are light and Jennie is darker."

Ned, age 12. "Sally." Why? "She's darker than Mary, and Mary is darker than Jennie, so she has to be."

What can we derive from this simple example?

A. Milo is not able to relate objects into an order.

B. Ned can operate on an abstract, purely verbal level.

....

A. Remember in the last chapter we saw several instances of elementary school children ordering objects or relating them in a series. The problem here is not one of ordering in itself, but ordering on a purely verbal level; therefore, read choice B.

B. This definitely seems to be true. Ned can solve the problem because he can think in abstract, purely verbal terms. Milo could have answered correctly if Mary, Jennie and Sally were all there in person—in the "concrete"—but when it comes to operating on a purely verbal level, he is at a loss. It is only the junior and senior high student who can understand relationships and solve problems on an abstract plane.

Closely related to the ability to deal with abstractions is another important characteristic of the thought processes of the secondary school student. See if you can derive it from the following exercise.

Problem #7. What do you think about this statement?

"I am glad that I do not like liver, because if I liked it, I would always be eating it, and I hate eating things I dislike."

Opal, age 10.   "I don't like liver either. It's awful tasting."

Pat, age 14.   "You can't say that. If you disliked it, you wouldn't be eating it."

What can Pat do that Opal cannot?

A. Distinguish the form from the content of a statement and evaluate the form alone, not considering the content.

B. Decide on a more substantial basis his preference for something.

....

A. Right. This ability to differentiate form from content is one of the key advances in the thinking of the adolescent over that of the child. It involves a "decentering" that only the adolescent can do. Whereas the child is limited in that he "centers" on or takes into account only the content of a statement, the adolescent can "decenter" his thinking, distinguish form from content, and analyze or evaluate the *form* of reasoning involved in a statement. This advance is so central to the thinking of junior and senior high students that Piaget called their level of thinking "formal operations."

B. What is involved here is not his decision regarding his preference for anything but his ability to analyze the line of reasoning regarding something.

For a further characteristic of "formal operational thought" consider another problem.

Problem #8. 15 is to 3 as 40 is to what?

Quent, age 10.   "I don't know. I know that 15 is equal to five 3s, but how do you find the answer to this?"

Rose, age 11.   "15 is to 3 as 40 is to 8."

What is Rose able to do that Quent could not?

A. Understand a simple relationship.

B. Understand a relation between relations.

C. Operate on a symbolic level.

....

A. Actually, Quent was able to understand a simple relationship such as the ratio of 15 to 3, but once the problem got more involved, he was at a loss. Check the other choices.

B. This is exactly what Rose was able to do—understand the relationship between two ratios or relations. In other words, she was able to combine two relations into a law, viz., the law of proportionality. Although the concrete operational child can grasp relationships, only the formal operational thinker can handle the higher order operation of relating relations into laws.

C. There is a lot more to the problem than being able to operate on a symbolic level. In fact, both Rose and Quent showed that they could handle symbols (e.g., 15, 3, 5), but what was Rose able to do in addition to handling symbols?

In the past few pages we have identified several other important characteristics of the preadolescent's and adolescent's thinking: the ability to think abstractly—to operate on a purely verbal, abstract level and to form abstract concepts; the ability to analyze and evaluate the form of reasoning as distinct from the content; and, finally, the ability to relate relations, e.g., into proportions.

We now get into some qualities of formal operational thought that are far from easy to understand but are essential to any complete grasp of Piaget's analysis of this level of thinking. Study the experiments and transcripts carefully, and you should be able to comprehend at least the essence of these important operations. We will analyze just two experiments, but each of them quite thoroughly. The first experiment is this.

Problem #9. A miniature "seesaw" is presented to the subject together with some 2 oz. and 4 oz. weights which can be put on the seesaw.

A 2 oz. weight is placed on the end of one side of the balance and the question posed: How can you balance the seesaw again?

Sam, age 10. "Take it off." Any other way? "Put a small weight on the other side."

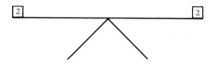

Can you think of another way? "Put two weights half way in."

How do you explain that? "You need two weights because it weighs less if it's closer in." How about if we put a heavy weight here?

"You could put a light weight on the [other] end." Why? "It's heavier farther out."

Tom, age 13. "Let's see, you could do several things to make it balance: put an equal weight on the other side, or put a heavier weight half way in on the other side." Why is that? "The shorter the distance, the heavier the weight has to be." How about this? How can you balance it?

"By putting a small weight at the end." Why? "The longer the distance, the less the weight you need. The length makes up for the weight."

Who is able to perform both forms of reversibility: negation and reciprocity?

A. Sam, who is still operating at the concrete level, can perform both (obviously Tom can also).

B. Only Tom can perform both negation and reciprocity since the latter requires formal operational thought.

....

A. Agreed. He certainly leaves room for improvement, but Sam does indicate—at least through the way he solves the problem, if not by explicit statement—that one variable (greater length) can make up for or compensate for another (lighter weight). He can, therefore, solve problems using reciprocity. He can also compensate for a weight on one side by putting an equal weight on the other, which is a more direct and simpler form of reciprocity. It is obvious, as well, that he can reverse through negation or inversion, i.e., by taking the weight off.

B. Granted Tom's ability to understand the operation of compensation or reciprocity is far superior to Sam's, but Sam still did grasp some relation between weight and length and was able to solve the problem, not just through negation, but also by allowing length to compensate for weight. Don't ignore choice A.

In relation to the same experiment, which of the subjects is able to coordinate the variables and see the proportionate relationship between them?

A. Sam (10).

B. Tom (13).

....

A. If you read his transcript again, you will see that Sam didn't coordinate the two variables to any appreciable extent. In fact, the one variable (weight) seemed to change—became "lighter" or "heavier"—as the other (length) was varied.

B. The ability to coordinate variables and relate them into a proportion does seem to represent a marked advance in the thinking of the formal operational student. The actual proportional relation involves the realization that decreasing the weight and increasing the length is equivalent to increasing the weight and decreasing the length, e.g., in the transcript: "the shorter the distance, the heavier the weight has to be; the longer the distance, the less weight you need." In terms of proportion (assuming that the length of either side of the seesaw is 4″) the relation would read: $2W : 2L :: 4W : 4L$ or by cross multiplying: $2W \times 4L = 4W \times 2L$, i.e., a lighter weight at a longer length is equivalent to a heavier weight at a shorter length.

It seems that both the concrete and the formal operational thinker can perform several transformations. For instance, in the seesaw or balance problem, they could certainly put a weight on one side (which we can symbolize by $+W$), and they could take away or decrease the weight, i.e., perform the inverse of the first $(-W)$. Similarly, they can increase the length $(+L)$ and also decrease it $(-L)$. What relation among these do our subjects—Tom more clearly than Sam—seem to grasp?

A. That the same result is achieved whether you decrease the weight or decrease the length; in other words, they realize that the inverse of one $(-W)$ can be replaced by the inverse of the other $(-L)$.

B. That the weights and lengths may be varied in most any way to achieve the same result, i.e., equilibrium can be achieved by increasing or decreasing weight or length on either side.

....

A. On the basis of their awareness of one variable making up for or compensating for the other—evidenced in both transcripts above—this seems to be the case. This process of compensating for one variable by the inverse of the other, e.g., reversing the effect of $+W$ by $-L$, is what Piaget calls reciprocity.

B. It's not quite as global and as random as this. For instance increasing weight *and* length on the same side of a balance won't result in equilibrium if, on the other side, only the weight *or* length were increased or if only one were decreased. See A for the correct explanation.

Can you discern another relationship among the variables?

A. Increasing the length (+L) has the same result as increasing the weight (+W).

B. Increasing the length (+L) on one side of the balance has the same effect as decreasing the weight (−W) on the other.

....

A. Right. The two variables +W and +L lead to the same result or "go together" in terms of their effect. You may recall from any smattering of statistics you have had that the "going togetherness" of two variables is referred to as correlation. This is exactly what Piaget calls this relationship, although he defines it (somewhat negatively) as the inverse of the reciprocal—which, if you analyze it, is identical to having the same result as the original operation.

B. You may be more of a concrete than a formal or abstract thinker. Imagine the effect on a seesaw if you *increase* a given weight's distance from the center: that side goes down more; on the other hand, if you *decrease* the weight on either side, that side goes up. Choice A reveals the correct relationship.

To review briefly, the types of operations that we have been examining are several: two types of reversibility, 1) cancelling out an operation (negation) and 2) compensating for a change in one variable by changing another (reciprocity); then, 3) doing something that has the same result or effect as the original operation (correlation); and, finally, we should specify 4) the original operation itself (identity).

Actually what we have been dealing with are the elements of Piaget's famous INRC group of transformations: Identity (I), Inversion or Negation (N), Reciprocity (R), and Correlation (C).

Recall our original transcripts in the seesaw problem and perhaps some of the subsequent analysis. What would you say the difference is between a concrete thinker (Sam: "It weighs less if it's closer in; it's heavier further out.") and a person on the formal operational level (Tom: "The longer the distance, the less the weight you need; the length makes up for the weight.")?

A. Tom was able to *handle* the different transformations; whereas, Sam couldn't.

B. Tom was able to *relate* the different transformations to one another; whereas, Sam couldn't.

C. Sam could neither perform the transformations nor relate them to one another.

....

A. Actually Sam could put a weight on one side ($+W$)—Identity; he could do the two forms of reversibility, i.e., Negation ($-W$) and Reciprocity ($-L$); and he even saw that the effect was the same when he increased the other variable ($+L$), i.e., Correlation. B explains the operation Sam was unable to perform.

B. Correct. This is seen rather clearly in our analysis of the proportional relationship that Tom was able to grasp. Sam was limited to doing the simple transformations one at a time, not seeing the relationship among them. According to Piaget, this is one of the great advances of the formal over the concrete thinker: that he is not only able to manipulate variables and transform his operations on reality in these several ways, but that he can understand the interrelationships among these manipulations and transformations and order them into a coherent whole.

C. Actually he was able to do one of these operations; so this is not an accurate response.

We saw earlier that at the formal operational level a person can understand relations between relations or proportionality, for instance, the proportion $W : L :: 2W : 2L$ or similarly $+W : +L :: -W : -L$. The latter can of course be written $\dfrac{+W}{+L} = \dfrac{-W}{-L}$ or by crossed products $+W \cdot -L = -W \cdot +L$.

In relation to the seesaw problem this would mean that:

A. the heavier the weight you have, the longer the distance from the fulcrum it needs to be.

B. the heavier the weight you have, the shorter the distance you need to keep a balance.

....

A. You are not following carefully enough. Remember the simple proportion $+W/+L = -W/-L$ or in verbal terms: an increase in weight on one side is offset by an increase in length on the other to the same extent as a decrease in weight is offset by a decrease in length on the other side of the fulcrum. This can also be stated $+W \times -L = -W \times +L$ or: a proportionally heavier weight at a shorter distance will balance with a lighter weight at a longer distance.

B. Right. Similarly the longer the distance, the lighter the weight you need (and vice versa in each case).

If, as we did above, we regard $+W$ as the basic operation (Identity) and $-W$ as its inverse (Negation), $-L$ as compensating for it (Reciprocity) and $+L$ as accomplishing the same result (Correlation), we could easily substitute the more general logical transformations for their physical counterparts. $\dfrac{+W}{+L} = \dfrac{-W}{-L}$ then becomes $\dfrac{I}{C} = \dfrac{N}{R}$ which means:

A. an operation is related to its correlative in the same way as its inverse is related to its reciprocal.

B. the correlative of an operation is compared to the inverse as the operation itself is related to its reciprocal.

....

A. True. Again picturing it in terms of the seesaw: the basic operation or $+W$ (I) and its correlative or $+L$ (C) have the same result, just as cancelling or $-W$ (N) and compensating or $-L$ (R) have the same result.

B. No. Try to work it over a little more fully. Remember that proportion simply indicates how two relations are related, i.e., this is to that as something else is to a fourth thing. Perhaps another source of the difficulty may be the abbreviations; remember that I is short for Identity and N for Inversion or Negation. Reread the question and try A.

If $\dfrac{I}{C}$ (or more concretely $\dfrac{+W}{+L}$) are related in the same way as $\dfrac{N}{R}$ (or $\dfrac{-W}{-L}$), then which combination would result in a balanced seesaw?

A.

$$\dfrac{I \cdot R \qquad N \cdot C}{\wedge}$$

B.

$$\dfrac{I \cdot C \qquad N \cdot R}{\wedge}$$

....

A. Correct. On the balance, Identity ($+W$) interacting with its Reciprocal ($-L$) is the equivalent of its Inverse ($-W$) interacting with its Correlative ($+L$). Or in the concrete again: a heavier weight at a lesser distance balances with a lighter weight at a greater distance. You can also figure it by crossed products, i.e., $\dfrac{I}{C} = \dfrac{N}{R}$ becomes $I \cdot R = N \cdot C$.

B. Analyze what this would really result in. You have two "positives" on one side and two "negatives" on the other or, more concretely, $+W \cdot +L$ versus $-W \cdot -L$. The balance is obviously going to tip towards the positive end and be out of balance (this is not exactly a multiplicative relationship and so two minus' do not make a plus). Rework the problem and try A.

Of course there are other ways in which weight and length may be interrelated. For instance, which of the answers completes the proportion: $+W : -L ::$

A. $+L : -W$

B. $-W : +L$

C. Both

....

A. Right. A heavier weight at a shorter distance has the same effect as a longer distance with a lighter weight. However, don't ignore response B.

B. Right. A heavier weight at a shorter distance is the equivalent of a lighter weight at a longer distance. If you haven't checked A, do so.

C. Agreed. For a brief explanation see the comments under A and B above.

If we take the proportion $+W/-L = +L/-W$ and generalize as we did above into $I/R = C/N$, then the relationship in terms of two factors acting together (which again can be figured by crossed products) is:

A. $I \cdot N = R \cdot C$

B. $I \cdot C = R \cdot N$

....

A. Right. Given the stated proportion it would mean—in concrete terms—that the basic operation (I or $+W$) combined with its negation or cancellation (N or $-W$) is the equivalent of its reciprocal or what compensates for it (R or $-L$) combined with its correlative or what has the same effect as it has (C or $+L$). For purposes of completion, besides the interrelationship $IR = NC$ and $IN = RC$, there is also $NR = IC$ derivable in the same way through the relationship of proportionality.

B. The INRC group is difficult but you shouldn't become discouraged. The best way to understand it is to go back and relate the more general, logical transformations to the more concrete, physical ones, viz., weight and length in the balance problem. The relationship $+W/-L = +L/-W$ would then become $+W \times -W = -L \times +L$. In INRC terms, which is the same as this, A or B?

_____

To sum up, one of the major advances that the high school student is able to make from the level of concrete thinking is, first, to fully understand the transformations of inversion and reciprocity (the two reversibilities) and, then, to group them into a single system such as we have been doing by relating them through proportionality.

The INRC group is so basic to Piaget's analysis of formal operational thought that it will pay to examine another experiment which illustrates both the transformations themselves and particularly their interrelationship. The experiment is this.

Problem #10. Two communicating vessels of different shapes are provided, one with a piston that can be loaded with various sized weights. Liquids of different density are also available: water, alcohol, and oil.

The questions revolve around the ideas of action and reaction of forces and the reaching of equilibrium. Analyze the following transcript of a junior high student.

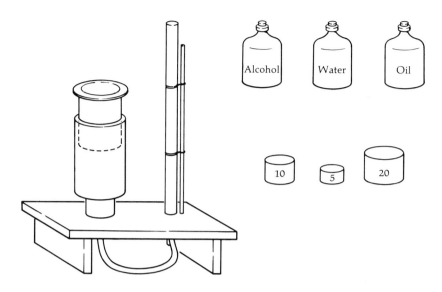

Vin, age 13. "The piston and the weights force the water down and then up in the other tube." Why doesn't the piston go all the way down? "It can't because of the force of the water holding it back." How about if we put another liquid in the system? "It depends on whether it's lighter or heavier than water. I think alcohol is lighter so the piston would go down more and the liquid go up more [in the tube]." Why? "Because it's lighter and has less force than water." How could you bring the alcohol down to where the water was in the taller tube? "By taking off some weight." Any other way? [No answer.] How about if we put oil in the system? "It [the piston] won't go down as much because the oil has more mass." How can we get the oil up to the water level in the tube? "Put on some weight." Any other way? "Take out some of the liquid."

First, what was the key to Vin's explanation?

A. The idea that the piston goes down as a function of its own weight.
B. The idea of resistance of the liquid proportionate to its density.

....

A. Actually this is how a younger child would explain the problem: "if the piston is heavier the water goes up [in the tube] more." The real key to a full explanation is B.

B. Agreed. The key to the full solution of the problem is the idea of the resisting force capable of acting in the opposite direction to that of the piston and weights.

The action and/or reaction involved in the problem and identifiable in Vin's earlier responses are/is

A. The action exerted by the pressure of the weight (of the piston and weights).
B. The reaction due to the resistance of the liquid (pressure in the opposite direction to that of the weight).
C. Both.

....

A. Right. He mentioned that "the piston and the weights force the water down". But is that all?

B. Right. He explained that the piston doesn't go all the way down "because of the force of the water holding it back." Check A if you haven't already done so.

C. Agreed. Refer to A and B.

There are also one or two transformations that Vin used in analyzing what was involved in the system. Can you identify it/them?

A. The suppression of the action of the weight by eliminating the weight.
B. The suppression of the resistance of the liquid by eliminating some of the liquid or by using a liquid of less density.
C. Both transformations.

....

A. Yes. This is obvious when he says: "By taking off some weight." See also response B.

B. True. This transformation is seen in the statements: "Take out some of the liquid" and "Alcohol is lighter so the piston would go down more." However, don't ignore the transformation in A.

C. Correct. For specific sources in the transcript, check the replies to
A and B.

These actions, reactions, and changes—and their directions—can be summarized as follows:

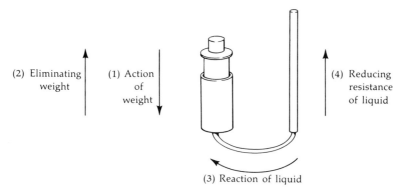

(2) Eliminating weight   (1) Action of weight   (4) Reducing resistance of liquid

(3) Reaction of liquid

If we consider (1) the action of the weight to be the basic operation
(Identity) and (2) the transformation of eliminating the weight as its
inverse (Negation), what are (3) and (4) in terms of the INRC group?

A. Reciprocity and Correlation respectively, because (3) compensates
   for and helps to neutralize (1) while (4) has the same result as (1).
B. Correlation and Reciprocity respectively, because (3) is in direct
   contact with (1) while (4) is in an opposite direction to (2).

....

A. Agreed. The reaction or force of the liquid offsets and makes up
   for the weight; more specifically, an increase in the density and "force"
   of the liquid compensates for an increase in weight (Reciprocity).
   Reducing the resistance of the liquid by lessening its density or
   amount accomplishes the same result or "goes together" with increasing the weight and, therefore, is its Correlative.
B. Sorry. Contact doesn't mean correlation nor is reciprocity usually
   in the opposite direction to negation.

The physical forces and transformations in this experiment then are really analogous to the logical operations and transformations I, N, R, and C.

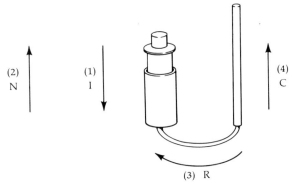

(2) N   (1) I   (4) C

(3) R

If you compare them, you will note different possible relationships among them. For instance, it is obvious that (1) or I and (2) or N are direct and inverse operations respectively; (3) or R and (4) or C are also direct and inverse operations in relation to each other, but act in the opposite direction from the first two. We have seen that reaction (3) is the reciprocal of (1); but also if you compare them, you will see that transformation (4) is a reciprocal of—makes up for—transformation (2), viz., lessening the density of the liquid compensates for and cancels out the effect of diminishing the weight. Another basic relationship is that two inverse operations, e.g., (1) and (2) or (3) and (4), cancel each other out; whereas, transformations in reciprocal relationship to each other, e.g., (3) and (1), (4) and (2), do not cancel each other but end up with the pressures equalized or in equilibrium.

If you understand these several relationships, you can see that they are prime illustrations of the formal thinker's ability to:

A. grasp the nature of the operations and transformations in the INRC group.

B. grasp the INRC group as a total, interrelated system.

....

A. It goes far beyond the understanding of the basic nature of the specific transformations. In this regard the concrete and formal thinker differ more by degree than in kind. See response B.

B. Agreed. In fact, these several inverse and reciprocal relationships provide an excellent illustration of the "structured whole" that is the INRC group. On the concrete level, the two forms of reversibility—inversion and reciprocity—plus the operations of identity and correlation remain separate and unrelated; on the formal level, they are integrated into a structured whole or interrelated system.

Before we review the many characteristics of the thought processes of the preadolescent and adolescent (and adult), try to recall the ages indicated in the sample transcripts in this chapter. About what age does a youngster begin to develop the operations and characteristics of formal operational thought?

A. Around 11—13.

B. 13.

....

A. On the basis both of your knowledge of individual differences among students and the transcripts of some of the younger formal thinkers presented in this chapter, you would certainly conclude that formal operations begin about the junior high level, perhaps a little earlier in some cases. This doesn't mean that formal thought appears full-blown, but only that it begins to develop. It reaches a level of relative maturity in senior high—around 16 or 17 usually. If you had any trouble understanding the INRC group, perhaps you could attest to the fact that formal operations leave room for further improvement up through the college years (and beyond).

B. Admittedly 13 was a common age in our sample transcripts, but we really can't pinpoint it that closely. A is a more flexible answer.

Review. We have attempted to identify the several operations and characteristics of the thought processes of junior and senior high school students by analyzing rather closely some fairly technical Piaget-type experiments plus sample transcripts. To review, the qualities of the thought processes of the formal operational student (11—13 through adolescence and adulthood) are:

Type of thinking	Hypothetico-deductive thinking: He can start with possibilities and reason or experiment from there.
	Abstract thought: He can form pure abstractions and think on an abstract, verbal level.
	Formal thought: He is able to distinguish the form from the content of a statement and consider the form of reasoning aside from the specific content.
Characteristics of thought processes	Verification: He has a need for explaining and providing proof or reasons for statements.
	Combinatorial system: He is able to think in terms of all possible combinations of objects, ideas or propositions, and also relate all of the possibilities into a "structured whole."
	Control of variables: He is able to isolate and control variables and operate on the basis of "all other things being equal."
	Proportions: He is able to relate relationships into laws or interrelationships, especially the relation of proportionality.
	The INRC group: He is able to relate the following operations and transformations into an integrated system:
	Identity (I)—the thing itself or the basic operation.
	Inversion (N)—the transformation which negates the basic operation.
	Reciprocity (R)— the transformation which compensates or makes up for the effect of the basic operation.
	Correlation (C)—the operation that has the same effect as the basic operation (or negatively, the inverse of the reciprocal).

Chapter 5

Some
Underlying
Concepts

Now that you have gained some awareness of the various characteristics of the thought processes of youngsters at various age levels, it is time to analyze some general concepts that underlie much of what we have seen so far, for instance intelligence, knowledge, and the causal influences that affect development.

Two very important concepts are illustrated in the next two problems.

Problem: Given the following figures indicate what is common to them.

Child: "They have four sides."

What he has done is organize them, group them according to their common element. His idea probably includes not only "four sides" but also, almost unwittingly, "symmetry," i.e., at least opposite sides are equal.

How would you characterize his mental operation?

A. It involves a grouping of objects according to one or more common characteristics.
B. It involves perceptual discrimination of positive from negative instances.

....

A. This is exactly what the child has done: put the figures that exist outside himself into a combination or grouping in his mind. In a word, he "structures" the objects in a certain way in his mind, i.e., into a classification of "four-sided figures." Piaget refers to this manipulating and incorporating of the objects in reality into a structure in the mind as "assimilation."
B. Actually, if you examine the figures, there are no negative instances; so it couldn't be B.

Problem. Some more figures are added to the initial ones. What about these?

Child: "They're four-sided too, but a little different."

He has incorporated these additional figures into his initial grouping or structure of "four-sided figures," but he also seems to have done something else. What?

A. He has discriminated between positive and negative instances.
B. He has changed his initial idea somewhat; on the basis of the new figures, he has dropped the "symmetry" aspect.

....

A. This answer still isn't correct since, even in the expanded collection of figures, there are no real negative instances. The new figures are somewhat different but are still included within the class of "four-sided figures" and, hence, are also positive instances.

B. Agreed. He has adapted his structure of "four-sided figures" to take into account something further in reality, the unusual, nonsymmetric four-sided figures. He has modified or accommodated his idea to bring it into accord with things as they actually are. Piaget calls this side of the interaction between mind and reality "accommodation."

On the basis of the example given would you say that assimilation is:

A. grouping objects into structures.

B. incorporating objects into existing structures.

C. both of the above.

....

A. It definitely involves this, as witnessed by the formation of the structure "four-sided figures." But even this grouping involved another facet of assimilation. Compare B.

B. True. For instance, the more specific structure of "four-sided figures" was incorporated into the *general* structure of the concrete operational grouping called "classification." Although the general structure might originally have been formed by working with specific objects such as figures, beads, blocks, etc., once it has developed, it becomes a general, underlying structure to which all other classifications are related. But this isn't the whole story; see A if you haven't already.

C. Correct. Assimilation involves either 1) organizing reality into structures or 2) incorporating objects or specific structures into other more general, underlying structures. For further explanation see A and B.

Do assimilation and accommodation seem to be separate processes or two sides of the same overall process?

A. Separate processes.

B. Two aspects of the same process.

....

A. Piaget thinks otherwise. To find out why, see B.

B. Piaget agrees. They are two aspects of intellectual activity, which is basically a process that involves interaction between mind and reality: we structure things in our minds but according to how they exist in reality.

On the basis of what you have seen in previous chapters, at what age would you say this grouping into structures is possible?

A. Age 5.

B. Age 8.

....

A. The average five-year-old couldn't form the classification of, for example, "four-sided figures" because he doesn't possess the basic operation necessary to do so.

B. True. By eight the child would have developed the concrete operations and especially the ability to group into classes which is necessary to classify the figures as "four-sided." The operation of classification then can be considered a general or underlying structure into which the specific grouping of "four-sided figures" is incorporated (assimilated). In turn, this underlying structure is changed, to some extent, through the addition of a new specific structure based on objects in the environment (accommodation).

Consider another example of a structure—the logico-mathematical structure of number—that develops through assimilation and changes through accommodation. Compare the simple concept of number that an elementary pupil possessed in the primary grades (1) with the structure that he has developed by the middle grades (2).

(1) Number—discontinuous quantity; remains the same through changes in arrangement

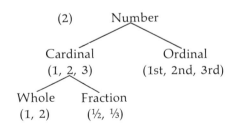

The addition of Cardinal-Ordinal and then Whole-Fraction to the original concept of number is mainly an example of:

A. assimilation.

B. accommodation.

....

A. Agreed. The new distinctions are simply incorporated into the general concept of number without a drastic change other than the development of the structure through further differentiation.

B. Although there is some accommodation, the example mainly illustrates the incorporation of new information into an existing structure, i.e., assimilation.

In this further development of the structure of number, something happened to the number 1 (for example). Previously, it simply represented one unit; now it encompasses both a unit (cardinal) and the first in a series (ordinal), plus it indicates a half, a third, etc., as the numerator of a fraction.

Which would you say this change is mainly an example of?

A. Assimilation.

B. Accommodation.

....

A. There is too much of a change for it to be considered assimilation. It's mostly accommodation.

B. True. As a result of the distinctions incorporated into the structure of number, one's conception of specific numbers is broadened considerably and takes on several aspects according to the new information acquired; in a word, accommodation occurs.

Consider the further development of the structure of number that usually occurs between the upper elementary grades (3) and the early years of high school (4).

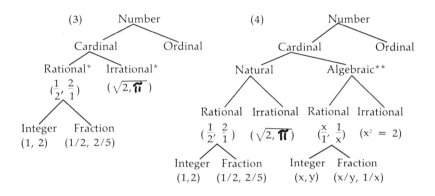

The addition of algebraic values to the third phase of the number structure, resulting in the fourth phase is an example of:

A. assimilation.

B. accommodation.

C. both assimilation and accommodation.

....

A. The new realm of algebraic values is incorporated into basically the same structure of number that the child had when he was in elementary school. The structure is further developed mainly by the assimilation of the new algebraic values. But this isn't all; see B and C.

B. The addition of algebraic values to the structure of number changes the whole concept of number from something definite (1, 2, 3, etc.) to something either variable (x, y) *or* definite. Hence, a whole new area within the concept of number is opened up. In addition, there are numbers that take on a different cast when expressed in algebraic form, e.g., $\sqrt{2}$ becomes $x^2 = 2$. Accommodation definitely occurs as well as assimilation. (Check explanations A and C if you haven't already done so.)

---

*A rational number is the ratio of two whole numbers, the denominator not equal to zero.
An irrational number is one that is not the ratio of any pair of whole numbers; it will never come out evenly if divided.
**An algebraic number is one that is variable, unknown.

C. Agreed. Most instances of the acquisition of new knowledge entail both assimilation and accommodation. New information is incorporated into an existing structure which is, in turn, changed to some extent because of the new insights and additional data. For why both aspects are involved in this instance, see explanations A and B.

What we have been talking about is basically "intelligent activity." In his *Psychology of Intelligence,* Piaget outlines several views of intelligence; which one would you say he holds?

A. "A system of responses to external reality."

B. "A conscious adaptation to new situations through a process of: hypotheses→trials→selection of what is empirically successful."

C. "A complex system of operations that involve genuine actions, i.e., a construction based on experiments on reality."

....

A. This is only half of Piaget's view, namely, the accommodation half. This definition is one held by many behaviorists who think of intelligent activity as involving a unilateral relation between environment and the organism, i.e., Stimulus→Response. Piaget's view entails a reciprocal relation, $S \rightleftarrows R$, where the input is incorporated into a structure (in the person) which, in turn, is changed in view of the demands of reality. Check the other responses.

B. This answer is close in several ways. First, it is a view held by the great European psychologist, Claparède, Piaget's senior colleague at Geneva (it is also a popular American view). Second, it involves some interaction with environment, which is important for Piaget. But it stresses adapting to environment too much, and it lacks one essential element (contained in C).

C. This represents the operational and "interaction" view held by Piaget. His view entails, on the one hand, *assimilation,* in which the data of reality are modified so as to be incorporated into the person's mental structures, and, on the other hand, *accommodation,* in which the mental structures of a person are modified and enriched because of the new experience with reality. This operational viewpoint has its roots both in 1) a biological theory of progressive evolution through interaction between internal and external forces and in 2) an epistemological relativism which describes knowledge as the product of an interaction between experience and deduction. See A and B also.

What about this word "structure" that we have been using so freely without really defining? Let's try to understand it better through some examples.

Situation. A social studies class.
Teacher: "You've lived in this city for quite a few years, and some of you have lived in other cities. What would you say we would need if we wanted to start a new city?"
Students give the following suggestions:
"Water and somewhere to grow food."
"A river or railroad—some way to get to the city and get out of it to other places."
"Some raw materials so that the people can make things."
"A good climate; you couldn't put it somewhere that's too hot or too cold."
"Some moisture."
"A source of power—water, coal, or something."
Teacher: "O K, we've identified what is necessary for a city; all cities should have these things if they are to grow."

What has the teacher tried to form in the minds of the students?

A. A basic concept of "city" including its main qualities and based on the experience of the students.
B. A list of particulars that some cities have.

....

A. True. The teacher has tried to have the students form a basic idea of "city," one that is derived from specific experiences with cities, and one that in turn can be used to incorporate the main characteristics of other cities into it. This is actually an example of what Piaget means by "structure"—at least physical structure. A structure in this sense is derived from our experience with objects: we organize the objects into an ordered and interrelated system of knowledge, i.e., into a structure. Once a structure is formed, other objects can be incorporated into it thereby 1) giving the objects greater meaning and also 2) developing the structure itself in some way—through further clarification, differentiation, giving it further support or evidence, etc. The above example of "four-sided figures" is another instance of the formation of a basic idea to which many things can be related, i.e., a structure.

B. There is something more to the teacher's plan than to just have the students list characteristics of cities; he wanted them to arrive at a realization that they are essential elements of a city. The relating of these particular characteristics into an overall concept of city is what the teacher obviously had in mind.

There is another kind of structure besides physical structure illustrated by the "city" and "four-sided figure" examples. We have already seen many examples of this other type in the last two chapters, e.g., the operational groupings of concrete and formal thought: classes, relations, number, propositional operations, proportionality, etc. For example, the concept of number was attained by placing stones or blocks or chips in a row, moving them out further, putting them in a circle, changing them around in a variety of ways; the child finally realized that, throughout all the different arrangements, the number stayed the same.

How would you say this type of structure is derived?

A. From the objects of reality in the same way that physical structures are abstracted from those objects.

B. From our actions upon the objects of reality rather than directly from the objects themselves.

....

A. These structures differ from physical structures in several ways, one of which is that they are derived from the ways in which we manipulate objects rather than from the objects themselves.

B. Correct. This second type of structure is not related directly to the qualities of objects; rather it is related to the ways in which we act on or manipulate those objects. In forming such structures we abstract, not the qualities of objects, but the properties of the actions that we perform on the objects, e.g., the property of *number* being conserved through all kinds of arrangements. Again, the underlying structure of *classification* is derived from the grouping action that children perform on various four-sided figures or on various cities or on different colored wooden beads, etc. The operation in common to all of these examples is that of grouping into classes. This operation, then, is seen to be an overriding or very general structure, specifically the structure of classification. Piaget calls this type of structure "logico-mathematical." It is derived from the actions we perform on objects, or, in a sense, from first-order physical operations. Some further examples of logico-mathematical structures are causality, time, space, system, possibility, the INRC group, etc. Needless to say, Piaget has mainly been interested in studying this type of structure rather than physical structures.

The logico-mathematical structures serve an organizing and inter-relating function for the physical structures that are derived from the objects themselves. What we mean by this is 1) it would be impossible to form the physical structure of "city" or "four-sided figure" if the underlying logico-mathematical structure of grouping into classes had not yet developed in the child, and 2) the physical structures of "city," "four-sided figures," "noun," "living beings," etc., are related in that they are all specific instances of the logico-mathematical structure of classification and are coordinated into this larger, more general structure.

_____

How does all this apply to learning? For Piaget, learning is the active search for and acquisition of knowledge. From what we have seen, what is Piaget's concept of knowledge?

A. A functional copy of reality.

B. An assimilation of reality into a structure.

....

A. Actually, Piaget is very much opposed to this view which follows directly from an associationist view of man's intelligence, which, as we saw a few pages ago, he rejected as too "one-way." His interaction concept of intelligence would require a concept of knowledge that is closer to B.

B. True. This concept follows directly from his operational view of intelligence as involving an interaction between the person and reality. Knowledge for Piaget is derived from action, i.e., the active assimilation of reality into the general coordinations of action (structures). To know something is to act on it, to organize and transform it, and, in this way, to incorporate it into one's cognitive structure.

With relation to learning, would you say that Piaget is more in the tradition of the Stimulus-Response or the Cognitive learning theorists?

A. Stimulus-Response such as Hull and Skinner.

B. Cognitive such as Lewin and Bruner.

....

A. Piaget was impressed with Hull's attempt to quantify learning and to construct a system with many intervening variables by which he attempted to explain the learning process, but Piaget himself hardly fits into the S-R tradition.

B. Piaget has many things in common with Lewin when it comes to learning, particularly 1) a biological rather than physical orientation since they tend to use biologically rooted terms such as assimilation and differentiation to describe learning, and 2) the use of "structure" as the central point in an explanation of learning. Although Piaget is primarily interested in the *development* of thought rather than in learning, he has contributed significantly to an understanding of learning through 1) a delineation of the concept of structure, 2) an analysis of the different types of structures: physical and logico-mathematical (also hierarchical, topological, and structures of order— cf. his *Structuralism*), and 3) an explanation of how cognitive structures are formed and changed, i.e., through assimilation and accommodation.

One final point before we get into the causal factors in cognitive development concerns motivation and the affective realm. On the basis of what you have seen of Piaget's work, which assumption could you draw?

A. He does not consider the affective side of man to be important.

B. He has not done much work in the affective area of man's behavior.

....

A. This is not a valid assumption; because he doesn't treat the affective side of man doesn't mean he thinks it is unimportant. On the contrary, he feels that motivation and the affective domain are extremely important; however, he has concentrated mainly on the cognitive domain. Read through B.

B. He obviously has done relatively little work in the affective realm, especially in recent years. *Moral Judgment* (1932) and *Play, Dreams and Imitation* (1951) are his two books that pertain to this facet of the child's behavior, but these are rather old and represent a small portion of his total work.

But this does not mean that he considers the social and affective side of man to be unimportant. Piaget claims that affectivity and motivation influence all of our cognitive behavior. In fact, the dynamic, motivating factors of love, esteem, self-actualization, etc., may well hold the key to our intellectual development. On the other hand, our cognitive structures help to give meaning to our affective states. Although one cannot be reduced to the other, and each can be validly distinguished from the other, the cognitive and affective realms of man are interrelated, interdependent, and even inseparable in actuality. In a word, even though Piaget has devoted his life to the analysis of the cognitive domain and its development, he still appreciates the essential unity of man's behavior. In fact, he has often pointed out the striking parallelism between the child's cognitive and affective development. But this is one of the many things that we are forced to leave out in this brief introduction to Piaget's thought. If you are interested further in this question, the best current source for his thinking on it is *The Psychology of the Child.*

What are the causal influences that are responsible for the development of the thought processes?

Recall the transcripts in the last few chapters plus your own experience with children and with yourself. Can you identify a sequence that seems to hold in all the cases you are familiar with?

A. Sensori-motor, language, intuitive thought, concrete operations, formal operations.

B. Language, sensori-motor, concrete operations, intuitive thought, formal operations.

C. Sensori-motor, intuitive thought, language, formal operations, concrete operations.

....

A. Agreed. Everyone that you or I know definitely went through this sequence of cognitive development. Until someone is found who proves an exception to this pattern (which is highly improbable), we can state that it is invariable. Even if you gave intensive instruction to a three-year-old, you couldn't teach him genuine conservation of number or quantity. Even if you set up a special training program in hypothetico-deductive thinking for the five-year-old, you couldn't get him to skip the concrete stage and go directly to formal operations.

B. This sequence would involve the "infant" (from the Latin *in-fans:* not able to speak) speaking practically from the beginning.

C. In the history of mankind there has never been observed a case in which formal thought precedes concrete thought!

What causal factor would you say this invariant sequence (sensori-motor through formal stage) is evidence for?

A. Maturation: the internal influence of organic growth.

B. Experience: an outside influence that includes interaction with both objects and other people.

....

A. Agreed. Not that maturation is the sole factor in the development of the thought processes, but it is a necessary and major influence, particularly in relation to the unvarying order of the stages of development. But organic maturation seems to become relatively less important as the years go on; whereas, the influence of experience—both physical and social—becomes relatively more important. As a child advances through the various stages, the age of transition from one stage to another varies increasingly. Whereas the symbolic function generally appears in different children within a range of six months or so, formal operations can appear as early as 10 or 11 or as late as the mid-teens (or even never for some people). The relation between maturation and experience seems to be that maturation continually opens up new possibilities which have to be actualized through exercise and experience.

B. Remember that, even with special training, you can't alter the sequence—which would indicate that experience is *not* the main determinant.

Consider the following situation.

Several children who are nonconservers but who are close to the age of concrete operations (6-7) are given some exercises to do:

Ten pennies are counted out on a table and then divided among them (3, 3 and 4). They are then told to put the pennies on the table once more where they are again counted all together (reversibility).

Two glasses filled with water plus a large dish are on a table. A screen is erected in front of the dish and then each child takes a turn pouring the water from one glass into the dish. The children don't see the change in shape, only the pouring—thus thought can be separated from perception.

A banana, an orange, a tangerine, a peach, and a piece of bread are given to each child; they are told to put them together in different ways (multiple classification).

Afterwards, the children are given a regular conservation test, and two out of three show that they can conserve quantity.

What causal factor would you say these exercises illustrate?

A. Maturation.
B. Experience with physical objects.
C. Social experience.

....

A. There really wasn't enough time for maturation to be the primary influence here; instead, it was experience, but which type?

B. Agreed. Active engagement with objects, as in these training examples, is an extremely important causal factor in the development of the thought processes. Although not sufficient of itself to explain development, such experience is absolutely necessary if a person is to advance from one stage to another. (You may know some adults who still operate mainly on a concrete level because they never had any experience with abstract, hypothetico-deductive thinking.)

It seems from the examples that children can be helped in their transition into another stage *if* 1) they are close to that stage already and 2) proper experiences are provided (the types illustrated have been found to be fairly effective).

C. There really wasn't much social interaction here. For the most part, it was physical interaction with coins, water, and edibles.

Consider the following situation.

A group of seventh graders with no previous experience with formal thinking is given the problem: What is the cause of elm blight? How do you go about finding what the cause is?

After a few guesses, someone suggests drawing up a list of possibilities; a few others offer suggestions for experimenting with the possibilities; one student stresses the importance of controlling the other variables while studying one; another student explains what they would be doing in terms of "if-then." Others ask questions; a lively discussion follows.

The next day the teacher gives a test item designed to measure problem-solving ability: drawing up hypotheses, testing them out, etc., and the students do quite well on it, much better than on a similar question he gave two weeks previously.

What causal factor is mainly at work here in the development of systematic formal thought?

A. Maturation.
B. Experience with physical objects.
C. Social experience.

....

A. Maturation is certainly involved on a long-term basis, but a short-term gain such as this is due to experience.

B. Experience with physical objects is not involved here as they hadn't had any physical contact with elm trees.

C. Right. Social interaction with peers, teachers, and parents is an important influence in the development of the thought processes, as witnessed by the above example designed to encourage the development of formal thinking. (Also compare the one- or two-year lag in cognitive development found in deaf children, who are somewhat deficient in social capacity.) But social experience is insufficient of itself; the child must actively assimilate his experiences into structures that he is capable of forming at certain phases in his development. In fact, too much "social transmission" by teachers is harmful because the child is kept from actively "inventing" structures and concepts and, therefore, kept from understanding them completely. In terms of social interaction, it is questioning rather than telling, devising materials and situations rather than demonstrating that are more appropriate for helping the child form the structures of a certain level of thought.

Besides maturation and experience—both physical and social—Piaget claims that there is another and even more important causal influence determining development. It is continually at work but is particularly in evidence at the time of transition from one stage to the next. See if you can discern what it is.

Situation: A child (age 7) and an experimenter are at a table with a ball of clay in front of them.

1) The clay is rolled into the form of a "hot dog" and the child says that it now has more clay because it is longer. (He centers on length.)

2) The "hot dog" is made longer and longer; the child says it contains less now because it is thinner. (He notices thinness.)

3) The long thin "hot dog" is brought back to its regular size and then lengthened again; the child admits that you can "lengthen" the hot dog. (He notices that as it becomes longer it becomes thinner.)

4) The clay is brought back to a ball, rolled into a hot dog, and then rolled further into a long, thin hot dog. The child says that the amount stays the same; the length makes up for the width. (He conserves quantity.)

What has happened in this sequence?

A. The child notices the different shapes into which the clay is rolled; he comments on the different shapes with particular reference to the length; he finally becomes aware of the relation between the parts and the whole.

B. The child progressively notices one and then the other dimension (length and thinness); he senses a certain connection between the two and notices the change in length; he finally realizes that the change doesn't make any difference in quantity since the two dimensions compensate one for the other.

....

A. Some of this is true enough, in a very general, superficial way. But the child does more than notice the shapes; he notices the two aspects of length and thinness and then the relation of reciprocity between the two. The part-whole relation doesn't really enter in as the clay is never divided into parts, just rolled out more. See response B.

B. True. The child seems to advance progressively all the way from denying that the quantity of clay is preserved through a transformation to the understanding that the quantity is conserved plus the reason for it (compensation of length for thickness and vice versa). The child reacted actively to some disturbances to his initial conviction of no conservation; he gradually corrected himself and finally arrived at a point of understanding and satisfaction (i.e., equilibrium). In the face of a conflict regarding his original explanation, he "righted" or—as Piaget says—"regulated" himself with the result that he attained operational reversibility, i.e., conservation together with the awareness of the compensation or reciprocity between length and thickness. This whole process of self-regulation is called by Piaget *equilibration.*

The process starts with a structure or way of thinking proper to one level; some external disturbance or intrusion on this ordinary way of thinking creates conflict and disequilibrium; the person compensates for the disturbance and solves the conflict by means of his own intellectual activity; the final state is a new way of thinking and of structuring things, a way that gives new understanding and satisfaction, in a word, a state of new equilibrium.

Piaget considers the process of equilibration by self-regulation the most important causal factor in the formation of the thought processes. "It is not an exaggeration to say that equilibration is the fundamental factor of development, and that it is even necessary for the coordination of the three other factors." [1]

---

[1] Jean Piaget, "Piaget's Theory," *Carmichael's Manual of Child Psychology,* ed. P. H. Mussen (New York: John Wiley and Sons, 1970), p. 726.

Review. The basic concepts that we have analyzed in this chapter are as follows:

Assimilation:	the incorporating of the objects of reality into a structure in the mind
Accommodation:	the modification of mental structures to correspond with objects in reality
Intelligence:	a system of operations that involves a mental construction based on one's experiments on reality
Knowledge:	an active assimilation of reality into one's cognitive structures
Structure:	an ordered, interrelated system of knowledge or operations that is abstracted either from the objects in reality or from our actions upon those objects
Physical structure:	an organized system of knowledge which includes a basic idea or relation at the core with other ideas, facts, etc., able to be related to it
Logico-mathematical structure:	a general, underlying system of operations or transformations characteristic of operational thinking
Maturation:	organic growth of the bodily systems, e.g., nervous, endocrine, skeletal, etc.
Experience:	interaction with the objects and persons in the environment
Equilibration:	the active process by which one responds to disturbances in his manner of thinking through a system of compensations; the result is new understanding and satisfaction, i.e., equilibrium

Chapter 6

Applications
in
Education

Now that we have examined the characteristics of the thought processes of both elementary and secondary school students and taken a brief look at some other basic concepts in Piaget's theory, it is time to make some applications to teaching from what we have seen. To some it might appear premature to apply Piaget's theory to actual classroom practice; they prefer to wait until a comprehensive body of research has demonstrated its relevance for teaching and the curriculum. Others—including the author—are willing to try out some possible applications even before all the evidence is in.

There are many reasons for this latter view. For one thing, Piaget's theory is by far the most compelling in the history of the psychology of cognitive development. Also, the preliminary case on the basis of both reason and research is strong enough to encourage a fairly wide application of Piaget's theory to classroom practice. The final case of course will depend on further experimentation as well as on the empirical evidence provided by teachers who attempt to apply his theory.

How can we apply to our teaching some of the insights regarding the qualities of the thought processes that we have identified in students

at various levels? We will proceed in a fairly chronological way, suggest-
ing different possible applications in a variety of subject fields. You
can make further applications to your own field of interest.

> Syncretism of understanding consists precisely in this, that the whole
> is understood before the parts are analyzed, and that understanding
> of the details takes place—rightly or wrongly—only as a function of
> the general schema.[1]

On the basis of the syncretism or wholistic approach in the preoperational
child's thinking, which method of teaching first graders to read would
you prefer (particularly for the large percentage of first graders who
are still in the intuitive stage)?

A. The sight-word approach in which the easiest, most commonly used
   words are identified and then repeated in simple stories.

B. The phonics approach which emphasizes the sound of letters and
   words resulting in an ability to sound out written words.

C. The language experience approach in which the children tell their
   own stories, the teacher writes them out, and then the children read
   them.

....

A. You might think that since whole words are learned, this method
   would be in keeping with the wholistic way of thinking of the young
   child, but words are really *parts* of sentences or stories. The sight-word
   approach is basically analytic rather than wholistic: it requires children
   to learn words (parts) first before they put them together into stories
   (wholes). There's another method that is more in keeping with the
   syncretism of the preoperational child.

B. The phonics approach is quite effective and results in a child's being
   able to read almost anything after a while, but it is still very analytic
   and "part-oriented." On the basis of the wholistic way of thinking
   of the preoperational child, this method might be better used later
   on rather than at the very beginning. See response C.

C. Agreed. In this way *whole* (but short) stories that are familiar to the
   children, since they wrote them, are read by all. If some children

---

[1] From *The Language and Thought of the Child* by Jean Piaget, Harcourt Brace Jovanovich,
New York, 1926, p. 162.

miss a word or two, it is not considered critical; they will learn them in due time. The important thing is that the method is in keeping with the way in which children understand communications (oral or written) at this level, i.e., they get the general idea and fill in for any parts or details they don't comprehend. More analytical approaches—phonics and sight-word—which progress from letters to words to sentences are appropriate at a later stage in reading instruction. The whole or language experience approach which proceeds in the opposite direction—from sentences to words to syllables—is more in keeping with the syncretistic, nonanalytic, sometimes subjective thinking of many six-year-olds. (Even if a child has already begun to do operational thinking, he doesn't necessarily switch all of a sudden to analytical rather than wholistic thinking; therefore, the whole approach would still be applicable to the early operational stage.)

Young subjects (4-6) seem to reason only about states or static configurations, overlooking transformations . . . [To them] a transformation . . . is not conceived as a reversible movement from one state to another, changing the form but leaving the quantity constant.[2]

In learning to read a language such as English in which the same letter can have several sounds and the same sound is sometimes represented by several letters, which method would you prefer especially for preoperational first graders?

A. The traditional 26 letter alphabet in which vowels have long and short pronunciations and some consonants have hard and soft pronunciations.

B. The Initial Teaching Alphabet of 44 letters in which each letter represents one of the 44 basic sounds in the English language.

....

A. The traditional alphabet requires the ability to conserve, i.e., to realize that A is basically the same thing even though sometimes it is pronounced Ā and sometimes Ă. On the basis of Piaget's findings, it seems reasonable to hypothesize that the difficulty experienced by

[2] Adapted from *The Psychology of the Child* by Jean Piaget and Bärbel Inhelder, Basic Books, Inc., Publishers, New York, 1969, p. 98.

many children, especially nonconservers, in learning how to read can be traced back to the fact that the traditional alphabet requires transformations that are confusing to the preoperational child. The significant correlations found between the ability to conserve and reading achievement tend to support this. Read through choice B.

B. The one-to-one correspondence between letter and sound in the ITA is much more appropriate to the preoperational level of many first graders. One of the main problems that these children face in reading is having to make a transformation in the sound of many letters of the traditional alphabet. The ITA doesn't require conservation (of letter) through transformation (of sound) or reversibility between phoneme and grapheme that Traditional Orthography demands. On this basis alone—to say nothing of the research studies and opinion of teachers—the ITA would seem to be preferable to T.O.

At about one and a half to two years, there appears a function that is fundamental to the development of later behavior patterns. It consists in the ability to represent something (a signified something: object, event, conceptual scheme, etc.) by means of a "signifier" which is differentiated and which serves only a representative purpose: language, mental image, symbolic gesture, and so on. We generally refer to this function that gives rise to representation as "symbolic." [3]

When could you start to teach a second or foreign language?

A. Primary grades or even earlier since the children possess the basic capacity to learn another language.

B. Middle elementary grades since by that time they have studied their own language sufficiently to provide a basis for learning another language.

C. Junior high since foreign language requires some of the characteristics of formal operations.

....

A. Agreed. What is basically necessary to learn a language is the "symbolic function," the capacity to let a symbol, e.g., a word, stand for a thing. Since this develops way before a child arrives in first grade, the learning of a foreign language could easily be one of the first

---

[3] *Ibid.*, p. 51.

subjects he studies in the school curriculum. The fact that many very young children actually *do* learn a second language also supports the conclusion that they *can* learn it on the primary level or even before.

B. Actually, a child doesn't have to use his own language as a basis for learning another. There are several more direct methods available that only require the basic symbolic or language function.

C. *You* may have waited until junior or even senior high to study a foreign language, but that doesn't mean you couldn't have learned it much earlier. Formal thought isn't necessary; in fact, it is probably too systematized for the easy learning of a second language. All that is required is something much more primitive than this.

> Number is a synthesis of seriation and inclusion. . . . This is why it is formed in close connection with these two groupings [of ordering and classifying], but as an original and new synthesis.[4]

Numerical operations require the awareness that 1 comes before 2, 3 comes after 2, etc., in a series and that 2 is really two units (1s), 3 is three units, etc. For instance, the operation of adding $1 + 2 = 3$ requires that a child realize the order of 1, 2, 3 and that $2 = 1 + 1$ and $3 = 1 + 1 + 1$. On this basis, when would you start teaching arithmetic operations?

A. First grade (age 6), since by that time children have learned to count and so can handle numbers.

B. Second grade (age 7), since most children are in the concrete operations stage of thought by that time.

....

A. More is involved in arithmetic operations than simple counting or even one-to-one correspondence, i.e., 8 8 8 8 seen as equal. If addition and subtraction are begun in first grade, many of the students—those that can't handle operational thought—will be lost and probably try to memorize or guess with the result that a negative attitude will build up toward mathematics that will be hard to overcome. B is a better response.

[4] *Ibid.*, p. 105.

B. If you had a nongraded system, you could begin whenever the children evidenced the ability to grasp the essential idea of number, i.e., that the number of objects in a group remains the same, is "conserved," no matter how the objects are arranged. But in a regular system, it is better to wait until second grade when most of the pupils are on the level of concrete *operational* thought before attempting to teach arithmetic operations. In the first grade about half the students will still be nonconservers and so will be confused—a bad way to start the study of mathematics.

If you found that some of your pupils, e.g., in second grade or in a nongraded primary system, were not able to understand addition and subtraction, what would you do?

A. Wait until they arrive on their own at the level of concrete operations before trying to teach any arithmetic.

B. Give them exercises in grouping so as to "tease" them into the operational thinking necessary to do arithmetic.

....

A. Recall that, according to Piaget (and many others), not only maturation but also experience with physical and/or social environment is a causal factor influencing the development of the several qualities of thought. So when a child is nearing the transition from one stage to another, you don't have to wait but can provide experiences that will help or challenge him into a higher level of thinking; therefore, read response B.

B. When a child is close to the transition to a higher level of thinking, you can encourage him into it by involving him in problems and exercises designed to give him experience in the next level of thinking. For instance, ordering each of the Cuisenaire rods from smallest to longest or classifying different cardboard forms into red and blue or into squares and triangles plus other problems such as those found in Chapter 3 will help the child acquire the basic structures of concrete operational thought and, hence, enable him to do arithmetic operations.

A word of warning is in order here, however. You should not attempt to tease students into the next level of thinking too soon. The research shows that "acceleration" is most successful when subjects are close to the next level. So if after a few tries some students just cannot perform certain mental operations, it is better not to force them but to wait a little before having them try again. Operational thought is much more difficult to those not used to it than it seems to us!

The process of equilibration or self-regulation is observable at the time of each partial construction and each transition from one stage to the next. It involves a series of active compensations on the part of the subject in response to external disturbances . . . and constitutes the formative process of the structures and transformations proper to a certain level.[5]

At the time of transition from one stage to the next, which would you suggest?

A. Providing conflict and challenge in the form of pointed questions.
B. Allowing the transition to occur as smoothly as possible without trying to accelerate it.

....

A. Agreed. Transition to the next stage is helped by some conflict and a realization of the contrast between one's customary way of viewing things and some aspects of reality that he has more recently become aware of. For instance, in challenging the child who is on the verge of concrete operations to classify things into living and nonliving, a teacher might provide experiences such as stories, movies, visits to zoos, etc.; ask questions such as "But how about a car: it moves, but is it alive?"; and finally, encourage discussion among several children on the question of what makes things "alive." The more disturbing the questions are to the person's customary way of thinking, the more he is apt to set in motion the whole process of equilibration.

B. According to Piaget, the transition from one period to the next is not really smooth but is characterized by disturbance and disequilibrium from which result the structures of the next stage.

---

[5] *Ibid.*, pp. 157 and 159.

The operations involved in the problems of conservation, reversibility, etc., are called "concrete" because they relate directly to objects and not yet to verbally stated hypotheses or propositions.[6]

What general emphasis would you favor in teaching youngsters on the elementary school level?

A. An emphasis on objects, experiences, visual aids, and field trips.

B. An emphasis on verbal explanations through lectures and reading.

....

A. This is clearly and directly an application of concrete operational thought. Although children can manipulate objects in their minds at this level, the objects must be related to the concrete, perceptible realm.

B. You've missed one of the main points of concrete operational thinking, namely, that the thinking must be based on concrete objects and events. Explanations are possible at this level, but the emphasis has to be on the concrete if real learning is to take place.

How about specific approaches in literature and social studies on the elementary level? Which would you prefer?

A. Stories, films; emphasis on persons and events.

B. Character analysis; causes, significant trends.

....

A. Reading and viewing films of some of the great stories in literature and studying some of the most important events and famous persons in history are appropriate emphases for the concrete level. Children should not just experience them but also be encouraged to grasp their essential characteristics, to classify them (comedy, tragedy, etc.), and to relate them in various ways (same-different, better-worse, before-after, etc.).

B. These emphases are more appropriate to formal operations than to the concrete level.

---

[6] *Ibid.*, p. 100.

Specifically in elementary school mathematics and science, which of the following would you suggest?

A. The abacus, Cuisenaire or Stern rods, geometric forms, games, nature study, weather study, etc.

B. Formulas, drill, information, etc.

....

A. These are obvious examples of concrete objects that are appropriate for elementary math and science. Children understand the computations of addition, subtraction, etc., if they use an abacus or rods (Piaget prefers those that indicate the units on the different lengths rather than the Cuisenaire rods, because they make obvious the various groupings of units, i.e., into 2 ☐ , 4 ☐☐☐ , etc., and they also deemphasize the color dimension that could be distracting to a child). Basic nature and earth study that emphasize characteristics of things, classifications, simple relationships plus the constancies in nature is most appropriate for the elementary level.

B. These traditional approaches are not really Piaget-based techniques; in fact, they are quite opposed to what he recommends, at least insofar as initial instruction in math and science is concerned. Formulas or recipes make for good computers, not mathematicians; constant drill and conveying of information might help train the memory, but it doesn't make even incipient scientists; A is the correct answer.

On the basis of Piaget's findings, can you teach grammar on the elementary school level?

A. No. Analysis of language demands a more verbal, abstract level of thought.

B. Yes. A concrete level child can handle the operations necessary for the study of grammar.

....

A. Actually, language analysis can be done on a first-order level and doesn't really require abstract thought. See choice B.

B. The study of grammar, whether from a traditional or linguistic approach, basically requires the ability to classify words or sentences and to relate them in various ways. Thus, it definitely seems that the concrete operational thinker, who can perform these basic groupings, can grasp the elements of language study or grammar. A comparable situation exists in the sciences, for instance, biology, where if classification, ordering, and the characteristics of organisms are all that are stressed, the elementary school child can certainly handle it. He is able to classify animals into land and sea, into mammals and nonmammals, etc., and he can even construct double classifications in which something can be two things at once, e.g., whale as a mammal and sea animal.

The Aristotelian and empiricist notion of induction, i.e., recording the data of experience and deriving an amplifying generalization, is an operation proper to the level of concrete operations.[7]

In the early phases of discovery and problem-oriented teaching in the elementary school, which would be more in keeping with the students' level of thinking?

A. Having students suggest hypotheses and work from there.
B. Having students collect data and work from there.

....

A. You would find that beginning with hypotheses would be a little ambitious for the reality-centered elementary school child. The approach in B would be more fitting for his level.

B. Collecting and examining data or objects and *inducing* a generalization from them is a very appropriate approach for the concrete operational child since he is oriented more to the real than the possible, to data more than hypotheses, to inductive rather than deductive reasoning.

Would you expect to find geometry included in a Piaget-influenced elementary curriculum?

A. No. It is a deductive discipline characterized by formal reasoning on the basis of theorems and axioms.

---

[7] *Ibid.,* p. 148.

B. Yes. The experience with geometric forms and their classification is both possible at this level and provides a valuable basis for formal geometry in high school.

....

A. Formal geometry certainly is all of this; but the experience with, measurement of, and comparison among various geometric forms can be included in elementary school.

B. Agreed. Children can measure different lengths and forms on the concrete level; they can classify forms as two- or three-dimensional or as three-, four-, or poly-sided figures; they can also relate geometric forms in various ways. All of this inductive experience will make the deductive study of formal geometry more intelligible. (Piaget notes that topological or "rubber-sheet" geometry is done by preschoolers; after 7 or 8, the intuitions of projective geometry and a sense of the Euclidean metric geometry are evidenced in children.)

One of the most central truths of the psychology of cognitive functions is that the development of the intellectual operations proceeds from effective action in the fullest sense, since logic is before all else the expression of the general coordination of actions.... The child's activity at certain levels necessarily entails the (internal) manipulation of objects and even a certain amount of actual physical groping, insofar as elementary logico-mathematical notions, for example, are derived not from the objects manipulated but from the actions of the child and their coordination.[8]

Which approach to teaching on the elementary level is more in tune with Piaget's theory?

A. Transmission of the knowledge and culture of a society by the teacher.

B. Investigation of problems and interaction with objects on the part of the student.

....

A. This approach is characteristic of receptive, lesson-oriented teaching which is more in keeping with the natural tendency of the adult's thinking rather than the psychology of the child's cognitive processes. Piaget is definitely opposed to this method in elementary school.

---

[8] Reprinted from *Science of Education and the Psychology of the Child* by Jean Piaget, translated by Derek Coltman, by permission of Editions Denoel, Paris and Grossman Publishers, New York, pp. 68 and 71.

B. These "active" methods that Piaget espouses are characterized by student inquiry and exploration of problems and by the spontaneous manipulation of and interaction with things in the environment and with materials provided by the teacher. This manipulation can be both internal and physical or simply internal. Examples of more active techniques are, for instance, role playing in the social studies, using the project method in science, and having students engage in creative production in English and the arts. These definitely represent the more appropriate approaches for the elementary level (of course, they shouldn't necessarily be limited to the elementary level).

Knowledge is not at all the same thing as making a figurative copy of reality for oneself, but it invariably consists in operative processes leading to the transformation of reality, either in actions or in thought, in order to grasp the mechanisms of those transformations and thus assimilate the events and the objects into systems of operations (or structures of transformations).[9]

For Piaget which would be more important in the study of, for example, elementary school geography?

A. An exact knowledge of what the main cities in the United States are noted for.

B. An awareness of how the main cities in the United States illustrate the essential characteristics of "city."

....

A. For Piaget, real knowledge is not simply an exact representation of reality, for instance, what the U.S. cities look like or are noted for. It's something that involves a genuine operation on reality, not just taking in a "copy" of it. B is the correct response.

B. This involves the child's doing something with the specific cities, i.e., coordinating them and relating them to the concept of "city." In Piaget's terms this means operating on the objects (specific cities), transforming them by grouping them into a structure or concept of "city" which stresses the basic and common characteristics such as

---

[9] *Ibid.*, p. 72.

water and food supply, transportation, access to raw materials, power, etc. When the pupil learns about new cities, he assimilates them into this concept or structure of "city." For Piaget this involves genuine knowledge which is far more than a simple representation of reality.

In elementary school mathematics, which approach is more in keeping with Piaget's view of knowledge as involving the assimilation of ideas and facts into a child's existing structures?

A. Relating a nickel to a dollar as 1/20.

B. Relating a nickel to a dollar as a quarter is to five dollars.

....

A. Correct. The elementary school child can grasp a relation such as 5/100 or by reduction 1/20, since he has already formed the general grouping or "structure" of the ordering or relationship among numbers. What is involved in the learning of a certain ratio is the assimilation of the ratio into the mental structure of the relationship between two numbers which a child has formed earlier at this level of thinking. (He has not as yet formed the adolescent and adult structure of proportionality and so cannot assimilate anything into such a structure.) In general, teachers must be aware of the structures available to learners at different levels of development—in fact, aware of the structures possessed by individual students—so that they can help them incorporate new knowledge into the cognitive structures that students have formed.

B. Not really. This would require a knowledge of proportionality which is an adolescent and adult structure rather than one that a child has formed at the level of concrete operations. A person must assimilate specific facts or ideas into the structures that he possesses, i.e., that are proper to his level of thinking. Compare A and B again and see if the answer isn't A.

Take another example from social studies. If you were to teach a unit on the American Indian to elementary students, which would you stress?

A. Characteristics of a hunting and farming people; the relation of the American Indian to the races of the Far East.

B. Reasons for their noncompetitive values; the issue of integration into the larger American culture.

....

A. Agreed. Again, to teach something to elementary students you have to relate the material to the (logico-mathematical) structures proper to that level, viz., classification, relations, etc. If you try to relate something to structures that you possess as an adult, your elementary pupils will simply not understand it.

B. These emphases call for logico-mathematical structures of hypo-thetico-deductive thinking that only develop in the formal operational stage. See choice A for the correct response.

The groupings of concrete operations are of two kinds and exhibit two fundamental forms of reversibility: inversion or negation and reciprocity or symmetry. The characteristic of negation is that the inverse operation combined with the corresponding direct operation cancels the whole thing out; the characteristic of reciprocity is that the original operation combined with its reciprocal results in an equiva-lence.[10]

When would you stress such things as:

In math: $32 + \square = 51; 51 - \square = 32$

In music: to give life to your singing, lower tones (pitch) should be sung with quite a bit of force (dynamism)

A. In elementary school since students can do both negation and reciprocity.

B. In junior high since only then can students coordinate the two types of reversibility into a system.

....

A. The first example is a case of simple reversibility by negation or inversion with its result being that one arrives back at the starting

---

[10] Piaget and Inhelder, pp. 136-37.

point. The second example is a typical instance of compensation or reciprocity whose end result is a situation equivalent to the original (e.g., singing that is "alive" through dynamism rather than the original high pitch). The concrete level thinker can perform both of these forms of reversibility. (It might be added that teaching complementary operations together, e.g., addition and subtraction, will help the child to think in terms of reversible transformations and hence to become more flexible in his thinking.)

B. Actually these examples call for the separate—not coordinated—use of negation and reciprocity. They don't really require formal operations; concrete will do. A is the most appropriate response.

The child discovers the conservation of substance and length at seven or eight. He develops the ability to conserve weight and the ability to coordinate horizontal and vertical axes at nine or ten. The conservation of volume develops at eleven or twelve. When adults try to impose [such] concepts on a child prematurely, his learning is merely verbal; true understanding comes only with his mental growth.[11], [12]

We have seen that Piaget's work offers many significant implications for teaching methods and approaches to learning on different levels, but how about its possibilities for curriculum development?

A. The study of the development of cognitive processes offers some broad, general suggestions but nothing concrete for the curriculum.

B. Piaget's research offers both general guidelines for the curriculum and also some specific indications of what should be taught at various levels.

A. Although we haven't delved into specific areas (space, time, number, etc.) in this brief introduction to Piaget, the above quote should indicate that his work provides something more than just general suggestions for the curriculum. In fact, he has a great deal to offer in this regard, as B will indicate.

---

[11] Jean Piaget, "How Children Form Mathematical Concepts," *Scientific American* 189 (1953): 74.
[12] Piaget and Inhelder, p. 99.

B. Actually, throughout the whole field of developmental psychology—and the psychology of learning for that matter—there are no
more significant indications for what should be taught at certain grade
levels than those found in the extensive work of Piaget and his
associates. If you are interested in examining this area more explicitly,
you would do well to look into an appropriate source or two in
the bibliography, e.g., *Number* and *Geometry* if you are interested in
mathematics, *Time* if you are or intend to be a social studies teacher,
etc. Most of these sources emphasize the elementary level, but even
secondary teachers can profit from them in that they will help them
realize what types of concepts students have already attained before
entering high school.

One result of a teacher's awareness of the specific capabilities of
the student at each age level is a more flexible and accepting attitude
toward assignments and projects. For instance in map drawing, elementary pupils advance from a topological stage in which general
relations are grasped (age 6-7), to an awareness of spatial orientation
but inaccuracy in representation (age 8), to the ability to draw full-
scale reproductions with only minor inaccuracies (age 10), to finally
the ability to draw proportionate representations, e.g., reduced scale
maps (age 12). A teacher who is aware of this gradual progression
will respect the developmental level of younger children and won't
demand perfect work from them.

Intelligence tends towards an equilibrium between assimilation and
accommodation. *Imitation* is the continuation of accommodation to
which it subordinates assimilation. *Play*, on the other hand, is a kind
of free assimilation, without accommodation to spatial conditions or
to the significance of objects.[13]

Play, intelligent activity, and imitation then are on a continuum in terms
of assimilation-accommodation, with play representing almost complete
assimilation, imitation almost complete accommodation, and intelligent
activity a balance or equilibrium between the two. In the classroom, would
you allow time for free play as well as imitation and "intelligent activity"?

A. Yes. Since assimilation is extremely important, time should be spent
in developing this side of intelligent activity.

---

[13] From *Play, Dreams and Imitation in Children* by Jean Piaget (New York: W. W. Norton
and Co., 1951), pp. 85-86.

B. No. School should be concerned with the learning of language (largely imitation) and the acquiring of knowledge and skills.

....

A. A Piaget-oriented curriculum would certainly leave room for free play in which students, even in high school, can experience what it is like to make space, time, and the other exigencies of physical reality completely subservient to oneself. There is enough imitation and pure accommodation in the curriculum; it should be balanced by some free play to give students a clear idea of what is involved in the very important process of assimilation. The play activities can be designed so as to give students a "feel" for operating on and transforming objects as opposed to the feeling of being inundated by models to be imitated and information to be remembered.

B. One problem with the traditional curriculum is that imitation plays too important a role, giving students the impression that human activity is largely a matter of adapting to environment.

The substructures of formal operational thought constitute a natural culmination of the sensori-motor structures and the groupings of concrete operations. It is not a question of adding another story to an edifice to which it bears no relation; rather, we have here a group of syntheses or structurations which, although new, are a direct and natural extension of the preceding ones and fill in some of the gaps left by them.[14]

If a high school student has not had previous experience with geometric forms or "unknown" quantities on the concrete level, what would you suggest for him as he begins to study geometry or algebra?

A. Have him go right into the formal study of geometry or algebra since he is on the level of formal operations and so can handle deductive disciplines.

B. Provide experience with geometric forms and graphic representations of "unknown" quantities before he starts the formal study of geometry or algebra.

....

A. The problem is that formal operations do not begin in a vacuum but build on the structures and experiences of concrete operations.

---

[14] Piaget and Inhelder, p. 131.

You may remember your own study of geometry: very probably you studied it in high school never having had any extensive experience with geometric forms previously. As a result—if you're like most of us—you didn't understand very much of it or certainly didn't retain much after your sophomore year.

B. This would support the point that Piaget stresses many times, i.e., that one stage of thought grows out of and builds on the previous stages. This would mean specifically for high school mathematics that basic structures (e.g., ideas of number, sets, form, relations, etc.) must be induced before a formal, deductive study can be embarked upon with any significant degree of understanding. For instance, if experience with geometric forms was not provided in elementary school, some time should be spent measuring, grouping, and comparing these forms before one studies Euclidean geometry. Similarly, some experience, before high school algebra, with squares of an unknown value, e.g., ☐ and one inch strips of the same length ☐ ☐ ☐ ☐ plus their combination ☐||||| will make the formal study of algebra, e.g., $x^2 + 4x$ much more understandable.

It is a confusion to think that any "activity" on the part of the student is a matter of physical actions, something that is true at the elementary levels but is no longer so at later stages, when a student may be totally "active" in the sense of making a personal rediscovery of the truths to be acquired even though this activity is being directed toward interior and abstract reflection.[15]

On the high school level which emphasis in learning and teaching would you think Piaget would advise?

A. Reception learning in which teachers convey information, concepts, and structured knowledge to the students who incorporate these into their previous (and present) knowledge.

B. Discovery learning, for instance, dialectical activities in which students compare ideas and positions, evaluate evidence, arrive at conclusions, and relate these to their existing cognitive structures.

....

A. Reception learning or verbally-oriented teaching is certainly more possible at the formal level and does allow more "ground" or material

---

[15] Reprinted from *Science of Education and the Psychology of the Child* by Jean Piaget, translated by Derek Coltman, by permission of Editions Denoel, Paris and Grossman Publishers, N.Y.

to be covered. The danger is that the ground is covered but hardly dug into, the material presented but not really understood or assimilated. Piaget actually favors more "active" methods.

B. Piaget definitely favors this more active, involved type of learning. According to him "all assimilation is a restructuration or a reinvention," i.e., in order to understand and relate something to one's cognitive structure, he must work it over actively and "discover" it for himself. The discovery approach can be either inductive, experiential, or dialectical. Induction and experience-based learning are most proper to the concrete level but, as we have seen, are still appropriate at the formal level for areas which are totally new to the student. The dialectical approach most befits the formal operational student and the hypothetico-deductive thinking, propositional combinations, and emphasis on verification proper to his level.

At the formal level the most authentic research activity may take place in the spheres of reflection, of the most advanced abstraction, and of verbal manipulations (provided they are spontaneous and not imposed on the student).[16]

The ability to operate on a purely verbal, abstract plane is definitely possible on the high school level. In the very practical matter of techniques of teaching, when discovery learning is not feasible, which of the following would be more in keeping with Piaget's thinking?

A. Formal lecture in which the teacher presents the material in an orderly way, and the students are questioned on it later.

B. Informal lecture in which the teacher explains something and the students react with questions and comments of their own.

....

A. The ability to think on a formal level doesn't mean that the student can be a pure "absorber" of knowledge, which tends to be the case in the teacher-centered lecture plus test approach. Therefore, B is the better answer.

B. This interaction between student and teacher provides for the "spontaneous—not imposed—manipulation" on the part of the student. Even on the formal level, a student must be active and work over the material, comparing, contrasting, questionning, requiring evidence,

[16] *Ibid.,* p. 68.

and ultimately incorporating the new ideas and relationships into his existing cognitive structures. While this is certainly not impossible in a lecture-test type course, it is much more probable when there is some interaction between student and teacher and especially among students and teacher.

There is one remarkable aspect of thought at the formal stage that has been largely overlooked because traditional instruction in schools almost totally ignored it, namely, the spontaneous development of an experimental spirit, which the combinatorial system and the propositional structures render accessible, once the proper occasion is provided.[17]

Which approach is more in keeping with the way of thinking available to the high school biology student?

A. Classifying organisms into a taxonomy.

B. Experimenting with the factors affecting the growth of organisms.

....

A. First, classifying can be done by the concrete level child. Second, science educators are getting away from a taxonomic approach and emphasizing an approach more in keeping with the capacity of the adolescent thinker—which is suggested in B.

B. This approach is definitely more in keeping with the hypothetico-deductive thinking of the adolescent as well as his ability to control variables and to examine all of the possibilities in a problem systematically. It should be noted that Piaget has found that this "experimental capacity" reaches a stage of equilibrium at about 15 or 16 and, hence, is more available to the senior high than the junior high student.

Which emphasis would you favor to prepare your students to perform experiments in high school science?

A. Providing demonstrations and detailed instructions for students to follow in their experiments.

---

[17] Piaget and Inhelder, p. 145.

B. Providing experience in hypothesis formation, selection of crucial variables, and if-then type of thinking.

....

A. This might provide a model for students to imitate, but it won't help to develop their experimental capacity. For this, more involvement and action on their part is necessary.

B. To use the genuine experimental method a student must be able—among other things—to form hypotheses, isolate and control variables, think in terms of if-then or mental experiments, and handle the other propositional combinations proper to adolescent thought. Experiences such as Suchman's inquiry training (short film demonstrations followed by student questions on the reason for the phenomenon—answerable by "yes" or "no"), if-then experiences such as city management games (given so much money, a certain population, and definite problems, what decisions should be made?), etc., are examples of approaches designed to develop the experimental capacity in students.

The adolescent is able to analyze his own thinking (propositional logic is a second-order operational system which operates on propositions whose truth depends on class, relational and numerical operations).[18]

One of the important abilities to be developed in the high school student is that of thinking critically about his own and others' lines of reasoning: to ask whether the reasons support a conclusion, or whether there are any contradictions or inconsistencies in a line of reasoning, etc.

Would you teach logic in high school?

A. Yes. Students can handle second order operations and analyze form of thinking as distinct from content.

B. No. Logic is best taught in college when students have greater intellectual maturity.

....

A. Adolescents can do formal and second order thinking and can analyze and evaluate the *form* of their reasoning. In a word, they can study

---

[18] From *The Growth of Logical Thinking From Childhood to Adolescence* by Bärbel Inhelder and Jean Piaget, Basic Books, Inc., Publishers, New York, 1958, pp. 340-41.

logic. The logic studied in high school should be more practical and the students more active than the typical formal logic course in college usually allows. It is important to note that if the analysis and evaluation of one's reasoning is not studied when the ability to do so develops, then it will be more difficult to engage in this second order thinking later on (the best time to fulfill any need or encourage any function is when it first emerges).

B. Students have the capacity to engage in this very important study in high school; why not provide them with the opportunity either in English or other courses or in a specific course in the analysis of the different types of thinking?

The later substage of formal thought (ages 15-16 and up) is distinguished by a new exigency which is absent in concrete thought and still implicit in early formal thinking: the need to find a factor which is not only general but also necessary, i.e., which will serve to express beyond the constant relations the very reason for these relations.[19]

Which would you stress on the high school level?

A. Character analysis (English); significance of events and decisions (History); proofs for procedures and solutions (Mathematics).

B. The relation between two short stories (English); similarity between historical and current events (History); direct and reversible computations (Mathematics).

....

A. Analyzing why characters in a novel act as they do, examining the significance and implications (cause-effect relationship) of historical events, and requiring students to be able to provide proof for each step in the solution of a mathematical problem are all approaches requiring students to get at the *reasons* for things, actions, or relationships. It is particularly senior high students who are intent on getting at the explanation, the necessity, or the proof for statements, but to a lesser extent junior high students are also interested in knowing the "why" of things. (Elementary pupils ask "why" but are usually satisfied with a "reason" that reflects constancy rather than necessity.)

---

[19] *Ibid.,* p. 11.

B. Relationships of greater or better than, of similarity and contrast, as well as the other basic operations and transformations illustrated here, are possible both at the formal and concrete levels. Aspects of thought found only at the formal operational level are described in A.

Propositional operations constitute an extension and generalization of the concrete operations . . . for a combinatorial system is a classification of classifications. The propositional operations, then, represent operations to the second power, but with reference to concrete operations.[20]

The same is true with second order *concepts* which combine two or more classes or relations arrived at on the concrete level.

Which concepts and emphases are able to be examined only in junior and senior high?

A. Comedy and tragedy as types of drama; expansion, direction, and other relational concepts.
B. Allegorical or symbolic meaning of stories and pictures; relativity or "mass as related to velocity and the system in which it is measured."

....

A. Tragedy and comedy are simply classifications—which a concrete operational child can grasp; expansion, direction, and other relational concepts are more difficult than regular concepts, but they can also be learned on the concrete level; therefore, B better explains the concepts appropriate for students in junior and senior high.

B. A child might get a laugh out of the face value of a political cartoon or follow and enjoy the story of *Gulliver's Travels,* but to grasp the allegorical meaning of the cartoon or the political satire underlying the story of Gulliver, one has to be on the level of formal operations. To understand allegory or symbolism a student must first comprehend the obvious meaning or theme (first order operation) and then comprehend what that theme or meaning symbolizes or stands for in another context (second order operation). The same applies for second order concepts such as relativity, density, mass, heat, volume, etc., which are formed by combining two or more first order or regular

---

[20] Piaget and Inhelder, *The Psychology of the Child,* p. 135.

concepts in some relational way, e.g., heat = mass x temperature, mass = $\dfrac{force}{acceleration}$ etc.

In its general logical form, a proportion is the equivalence of the relations connecting two terms to the relations connecting two other terms. . . . The notion of logical proportions is inherent in the integrated structure which seems to dominate the acquisitions specific to the level of formal operations.[21]

Mathematical proportions, e.g., 5 : 15 :: 20 : 60, are one type of proportion; but there are others used in the humanities, for instance, analogies, similies, and metaphors.

Recall our music example; which of the following could the formal operational—but not the concrete—student grasp?

A. To make a piece of music lively, lower notes have to be sung with more force; if they are not, they will sound dull.

B. In terms of dynamism in a piece of music, a higher note sung with less intensity is equivalent to a lower note sung with greater intensity.

....

A. There is not much here that couldn't be grasped by the concrete thinker: all that is involved is a simple relationship, not a proportion. B illustrates proportionality.

B. Right. It takes a formal operational thinker to combine two relations into a further relation of equivalence—which is the same thing as proportionality. Another example in the arts would be the proportionate relation between color and expanse, i.e., a bright color used sparingly would provide as much "life" to a painting as a pastel shade used more fully. You might try to think of further examples in your own field.

The INRC group is of psychological importance because it actually corresponds to certain fundamental structures of thought at the formal

---

[21] Inhelder and Piaget, *The Growth of Logical Thinking,* pp. 314-15.

level, particularly negation and symmetry. At this level the subject can both distinguish and coordinate [into a single system] inversions, reciprocities and correlativities (inversions: e.g., increase or diminish a force in one of the parts of the system; reciprocities: e.g., compensate for a force by an equivalent force, thus assuring symmetry between the parts; correlativities: reciprocity in negation).[22]

Consider a simple example of the INRC group in social studies. There is a problem of malnutrition in certain lower income sections of the city because of the relatively high cost of more nourishing foods (Identity). One possible solution is a food program: surplus foods and instruction on how to get more food value for the same amount of money (Negation). Another solution offered is the institution of a legal aid service that will help the people get fairer rents from their landlords—which would provide more money for food (Reciprocity). In addition, a program might be instituted that would emphasize an awareness of the cultural background, the humor and creativity, to say nothing of the low incidence of heart ailments because of being over-weight, that many lower income persons have (Correlation).

What type of questions could you ask high school students realizing that they can relate I, N, R and C into a coordinated group (or perhaps to help them coordinate these transformations into a single system)?

A. How will the food program solve the problem? How could a legal aid service help to solve the problem of malnutrition?

B. How are the three solutions similar, how different? Which would be more effective and why?

....

A. Actually even elementary students could answer these questions since they deal with negation and reciprocity separately. The advance possible on the high school level is that students can relate these transformations into a coordinated system. See B.

B. Correct. In this way various relationships among the solutions can be drawn, e.g., the food program and legal aid solutions would accomplish the same result and, therefore, are correlative to one another; the cultural background and lack of heart disease proposal is not a solution but a correlative of the original problem and to some extent the reciprocal of the food program solution.

[22] *Ibid.*, p. 134.

Similarly in history, government, and geography on the high school level, students can comprehend the continual interplay of environmental forces and human decisions, and the balance of powers among nations and men, all of which involve various compensations and cancellations. For instance in history, one country might possess a strong military force which another country can negate through a treaty or compensate for by an equivalent force or a force with less men but more advanced weaponry. In the same context, various relationships and compensations can be examined: military, economic, geographic, etc.

In literature, a passage or phrase can have a direct and obvious meaning (identity); irony and antithesis would represent the inverse of a direct statement ("cold comfort," "war is kind," etc.); contrast and paradox compensate or make up for the force of a direct statement by providing a "force" in the opposite direction (reciprocity); finally, correlation can be illustrated by the underlying relationship of two contexts or levels of description, e.g., a woman and her actions described in terms of a tigress.

In the study of literature (and comparably in other subjects), what can a teacher emphasize with high school students that will increase their understanding and ability to interpret passages and phrases more than is possible with younger children?

A. Comparisons among the several types of figures of speech or "transformations" in literature.

B. The identification and illustration of the several forms of imagery in poetry and prose.

....

A. Again, the significant advance evidenced in the adolescent is his ability to coordinate the different transformations of thought into a single system, i.e., to grasp the comparisons and other relationships among them. An emphasis on this way of thinking as it applies in literature, science, math, social sciences, etc., will raise the student's level of comprehension and sophistication. Whether explicit training is given in the complex thinking reflected in the INRC group as a preparation for this more advanced kind of analysis and comprehension, or whether such experience is provided in the context of literature, science, etc., doesn't matter as much as the fact that an opportunity for awareness and practice in this type of thinking is given to the high school student at some point in the curriculum.

B. Even upper elementary pupils can grasp some of the simpler, nonproportionate types of imagery such as contrast and irony. Choice B describes the method of study possible with high school students.

The method adopted by Piaget aims at an analysis of the different qualitative forms of intellectual development. It attempts to identify them and to evaluate their internal consistency. It is somewhat analogous to the experimental method used in studies of problem solving in that it uses apparatus and to the interview method in that it involves discussion with the subject. This aspect, the discussion, plays an important role in that it enables the experimenter to grasp the type of reasoning that underlies the child's conduct.[23]

Before we leave the topic of applications to education, we should examine one final point regarding the method that Piaget uses in his studies. His *qualitative* approach to the study of mental development with its use of the half-experiment, half-interview "clinical" method is quite different from the *quantitative* approach which uses general intelligence or multiple aptitude tests. Piaget's approach gets at the kinds of operations and the characteristics of thought processes at different levels; whereas, the psychometric or intelligence test approach shows mainly that as children get older they are able to answer more questions on a test.

Which technique would be more useful as a measure of readiness for learning—especially in the primary grades and junior high?

A. Piaget's clinical method.

B. A multiple aptitude test.

....

A. The clinical method with its facility to identify the operations and structures that children have developed at certain levels is a much more useful technique for determining whether a student has the

[23] From "The Study of Problem Solving and Thinking," by Bärbel Inhelder and Benjamin Matalon in *Handbook of Research Methods in Child Development*, Paul H. Mussen, ed. (New York: John Wiley and Sons, 1960), p. 448.

necessary capacity to grasp different areas of study and handle different approaches to learning. In a word, it is a better measure of
readiness for learning. It is also valuable for identifying sources of
difficulty in certain subjects especially reading, mathematics, and
science. Regular aptitude tests measure how you compare with others
on some basic intellectual abilities—verbal, quantitative, spatial,
etc.—and also offer an approximate prediction of how well a student
will do in various subjects. Although both have their purpose and
value in the school, in terms of readiness and diagnosis, the clinical
method is much more valuable.

B. The psychometric approach—especially if multiple aptitude tests are
used—provides valuable data, e.g., some indication of probable degree
of success in school and an idea of inter- and intra-individual variation
in basic types of abilities. But such tests don't reveal as much as
do the Piaget-type measures concerning the degree to which an
individual possesses the operations and qualities of thought necessary
to handle many schools subjects. Piaget's clinical method offers more
as far as readiness is concerned.

This will have to suffice for our examination of some of the implications
of Piaget's theory for teaching and the curriculum, especially in the
humanities, the social sciences, and mathematics. If we seem to have
slighted the sciences, it is simply because most of the problems used
in previous chapters—and used by Piaget himself—provide sufficient
illustrations of how an awareness of the thought processes could be
applied in the context of the sciences, particularly the physical sciences.

The applications suggested here are, for the most part, those that can
be derived from the general aspects of Piaget's theory that we have
examined in the earlier parts of this "guide." More specific applications
are certainly possible in the several subject fields; to get further ideas
on how his theory and research might be applied to your specific field,
check into some of the sections of Athey and Rubadeau (1970) and
under Piaget in the past ten years or so of *Education Index.*

A capsule review of the many applications we have made is in order
here. We have grouped them under several headings: general approaches
in the curriculum, placement of subjects, helping the thought processes
to develop, teaching strategies, and measurement. Within each category,
we have indicated the approach suggested, the subject or level, and finally
the basis for the application.

1. General Approaches in the Curriculum

Approach	Subject/Level	Basis	Page
language experience	reading	syncretism	78
ITA	reading	preoperational level	79
specifics, classes, relations	English, social studies	concrete operations	84
concrete objects	math, science	concrete operations	85
structure	geography	knowledge as assimilating into structures	88
relating to structures	mathematics	knowledge as assimilating into structures	89
relating to structures	social studies	knowledge as assimilating into structures	89
reversibility	math, music, etc.	negation & reciprocity	90
free play	all levels	assimilation	92
prerequisites	mathematics	each stage based on previous stages	93
experimentation	science	experimental capacity	96
reasons, necessity	several subjects	verification	98
second order concepts	several subjects	second order operations	99
proportions	arts, math	proportionality	100
coordination of transformations	social studies	INRC group	100
coordination of transformations	literature	INRC group	102

2. Placement of Subjects in the Curriculum

Subject	Level	Basis	Page
foreign language	primary	symbolic function	80
arithmetic	grade two	operational thought	81
grammar	elementary level	concrete operations	85
geometry	elementary level	concrete operations	86
specific topics	mainly elementary	different rate of development	91
logic	secondary	formal thought	97

3. Helping the Development of the Thought Processes

Approach	Reason	Page
experiences in grouping	transition to concrete operations	82
conflict and challenge	transition from one stage to next	83
experiences in hypothesis formation, etc.	training for experimental capacity	96

4. Teaching Strategies

Approach	Level	Basis	Page
concrete approaches	elementary	concrete operations	84
emphasis on data, induction	elementary	inductive reasoning	86
active methods	elementary	manipulation of objects	87
discovery	secondary	learning as an active process	94
explanation with interaction	secondary	learning as an active process	95

5. Measurement

Purpose	Reason	Page
readiness for learning	qualitative, clinical method	103

Postscript

The purpose of this discovery guide to Piaget has been to provide a basic introduction to the thought of the leading developmental psychologist in the world today. If it furnishes a background to make your reading of Piaget himself more comprehensible, then it will have been a success.

How significant is Piaget's theory and research? I would suggest that it is too early to make a definitive judgment regarding his theory, for he is continually refining it, assimilating new research data into it, and accommodating it to the new data. However, even at this point he has inspired almost as much research and commentary as have Freud in dynamic psychology and Hull in the psychology of learning. The purpose of this introduction was to present his thought rather than criticize it, to help you gain an understanding rather than offer an evaluation. (For some tentative critiques of his work you might consult Baldwin or Flavell in the bibliography.)

Piaget is sufficiently committed to truth that he will probably welcome the day when his theory of cognitive development is surpassed by another, more penetrating one. But to date in the field of developmental psychology, there exists a no more significant theory both for the understanding of the thought processes and for applications to classroom teaching than that of Jean Piaget.

The
Stages
of
Cognitive
Development

0 to 2*   Sensori-motor

                   sensori-motor reflexes and habits
                   awareness of permanent object
                   use of means to gain ends

2 to 4   Symbolic thought

                   language
                   symbolic play

4 to 7   Intuitive thought

                   syncretism of understanding
                   transductive reasoning

---

* All ages represent approximate averages

7 to 12   Concrete operations

                           classifying and ordering

                           decentering and coordination

                           reversibility

                           inductive reasoning

12 and up   Formal operations

                           hypothetico-deductive thinking

                           abstract and formal thought

                           all possible combinations

                           control of variables

                           verification of statements

                           proportionality

                           integrated system of operations and transformations

Glossary—Index

111

Bibliography

Books by Jean Piaget

The language and thought of the child. New York: Harcourt Brace Jovanovich, 1926.

Judgment and reasoning in the child. New York: Harcourt Brace Jovanovich, 1928.

The child's conception of the world. New York: Harcourt Brace Jovanovich, 1929.

The child's conception of physical causality. London: Kegan Paul, 1930.

The moral judgment of the child. London: Kegan Paul, 1932.

The psychology of intelligence. New York: Harcourt Brace Jovanovich, 1950.

Play, dreams and imitation in children. New York: W. W. Norton & Co., 1951.

The child's conception of number. New York: Humanities Press, 1952.

The origins of intelligence in children. New York: International Universities Press, 1952.

The construction of reality in the child. New York: Basic Books, Inc., Publishers, 1954.

Logic and psychology. New York: Basic Books, Inc., Publishers, 1957.

Six psychological studies (D. Elkind, Ed.). New York: Random House, 1967.

The child's conception of time. New York: Basic Books, Inc., Publishers, 1969.

The mechanisms of perception. New York: Basic Books, Inc., Publishers, 1969.

The child's conception of movement and speed. New York: Basic Books, Inc., Publishers, 1970.

Science of education and the psychology of the child. Translated by Derek Coltman, New York: Grossman Publishers, Orion Press, 1970.

Structuralism. New York: Basic Books, Inc., Publishers, 1970.

Books by Jean Piaget and Bärbel Inhelder

The child's conception of space. London: Routledge & Kegan Paul, 1956.

The growth of logical thinking from childhood to adolescence. New York: Basic Books, Inc., Publishers, 1958.

The child's conception of geometry. New York: Basic Books, Inc., Publishers, 1960.

The early growth of logic in the child. New York: Harper & Row, 1964.

The psychology of the child. New York: Basic Books, Inc., Publishers, 1969.

Articles in English by Piaget

"The right to education in the modern world." In *UNESCO, Freedom and culture.* New York: Columbia University Press, 1951, 67-116.

"How children form mathematical concepts." *Scientific American* 189 (1953): 74-78.

"Perceptual and cognitive (or operational) structures in the development of the concept of space in the child." *Acta Psychologica* 11 (1955): 41-46.

"The development of time concepts in the child." In *Psychopathology of childhood,* edited by R. H. Hoch and J. Zubin. New York: Grune & Stratton, 1955, 34-44.

"The child and modern physics." *Scientific American* 196 (1957): 46-51.

"Principal factors determining intellectual evolution from childhood to adult life." In *Outside readings in psychology,* 2nd ed., edited by E. L. Hartley and R. E. Hartley. New York: Thomas Y. Crowell Co., 1958, 43-55.

"The genetic approach to the psychology of thought." *Journal of Educational Psychology* 52 (1961): 275-281.

"Comments on Vygotsky's critical remarks concerning *The language and thought of the child* and *Judgment and reasoning in the child.*" In *Thought and language,* L. S. Vygotsky. Cambridge, Mass.: M.I.T. Press, 1962.

"The attainment of invariance and reversible operations in developmental thinking." *Social Research* 30 (1963): 283-299.

"Development and learning." *Journal of Research in Science Teaching* 2 (1964): 176-186.

"Piaget's theory." In *Carmichael's manual of child psychology*, edited by P. H. Mussen. New York: John Wiley and Sons, 1970, 703-732.

Secondary Sources

Almy, M. *Young children's thinking: studies of some aspects of Piaget's theory.* New York: Teachers College Press, 1966.

Athey, I. J., and Rubadeau, D. O., eds. *Educational implications of Piaget's theory.* Waltham, Mass.: Ginn-Blaisdell, 1970.

Baldwin, A. L. *Theories of child development.* New York: John Wiley and Sons, 1967.

Beard, R. M. *An outline of Piaget's developmental psychology for students and teachers.* New York: Basic Books, 1969.

Boyle, D. G. *A students' guide to Piaget.* Elmsford, N.Y.: Pergamon Press, 1969.

Brearley, M., ed. *The teaching of young children: some applications of Piaget's learning theory.* New York: Schocken Books, 1969.

Brearley, M., and Hitchfield, E. *A guide to reading Piaget.* New York: Schocken Books, 1966

Copeland, R. W. *How children learn mathematics: teaching implications of Piaget's research.* New York: The Macmillan Co., 1970.

Elkind, D. *Children and adolescents: interpretative essays on Jean Piaget.* New York: Oxford University Press, 1970.

Elkind, D., and Flavell, J., eds. *Studies in cognitive development: essays in honor of Jean Piaget.* New York: Oxford University Press, 1969.

Flavell, J. *The developmental psychology of Jean Piaget.* Princeton: Van Nostrand, 1963.

Furth, H. G. *Piaget and knowledge.* Englewood Cliffs, N. J.: Prentice-Hall, 1969.

Furth, H. G. *Piaget for teachers.* Englewood Cliffs, N. J.: Prentice-Hall, 1970.

Ginsburg, H., and Opper, S. *Piaget's theory of intellectual development.* Englewood Cliffs, N.J.: Prentice-Hall, 1969.

Lovell, K. *The growth of basic mathematical and scientific concepts in children.* London: University of London Press, 1961.

Phillips, J. L. *The origins of intellect: Piaget's theory.* San Francisco: Freeman, 1969.

Ripple, R. E., and Rockcastle, V. N., eds. *Piaget rediscovered.* Ithaca, N. Y.: Cornell University Press, 1964.

Sigel, I. E., and Hooper, F. H. *Logical thinking in children: research based on Piaget's theory.* New York: Holt, Rinehart & Winston, 1968.